THE UNTOLD STORY *of* KAKORI

TRAIN DACOITY TO LOOT BRITISH MONEY THAT HAPPENED ON 9TH AUGUST, 1925

SMITA DHRUV

PRABHAT
PAPERBACKS

Published by

PRABHAT PAPERBACKS

An Imprint of Prabhat Prakashan Pvt. Ltd.
4/19 Asaf Ali Road,
New Delhi–110 002 (INDIA)
e-mail: prabhatbooks@gmail.com

ISBN 978-93-5521-254-2
THE UNTOLD STORY OF KAKORI
by Smita Dhruv

Edition
2022

Price
₹ 400 (Rupees Four Hundred Only)

Printed at
Sanjay Printer, Sahibabad

Rest in peace, Kakori Boys!
Your sacrifices shall not go wasted.

कस ली है कमर अब तो, कुछ करके दिखाँएगें,
आज़ाद ही हो लेंगे, या सर ही कटा देंगे।

–अशफ़ाक़ उल्ला खाँ

यह सच है मौत हमको मिटा देगी एक दिन,
लेकिन हमारा नाम मिटाया न जाएगा।

–पं. रामप्रसाद बिस्मिल

To my dear husband Amal,
whose constant support has made this book possible

Foreword

The Great Freedom Fighters

'Destination Kakori: 9th August, 1925' is blessed by families of the legends of India's Freedom Struggle, whose contribution is unparalleled in the Indian history.

1.Chaphekar Ji Bandhu (1870 s - 1899)

Chaphekarr Bandhus-Damodar Ji, Balkrishna Ji and Vasudeo Ji's brave and fearless fight against the British soon after the war of 1857 can never be forgotten. Their dedication and clever approach in taking the British Government head-on, always remained an inspiration to the next generation of revolutionaries such as Veer Savarkar, Chandrashekhar Azad, Ramprasad Bismil, Bhagat Singh and many others. Every Indian is proud of the heritage they left for us. They climbed the gallows with a smile.

2.Shivram Ji Hari Rajguru (1908 - 1931)

Shivram Ji Hari Rajguru needs no introduction to any Indian of the independent India. Shivram Ji, a sharp shooter, was always eager to put himself first in any dangerous situation while fighting against the British Government. Thus, he climbed the gallows, along with Bhagat Singh Ji and Sukhdev Ji to become immortal in the history of India's freedom struggle.

3.Shachindra Nath Ji Bakshi (1900 - 1984)

Shachindra Nath Ji Bakshi was born in an affluent Bengali family. He chose to give up a luxurious life in the British India and became a revolutionary to fight for the country's freedom. His intelligence and sharp wit made him very popular and respected among his team of 'Hindustan Republican Association.' He was one of the ten bravehearts who participated in the great Kakori Conspiracy, and was sentenced to life imprisonment.

By Chetan Ji Chaphekar (Chaphekar Bandhu's great grandson)

'Destination Kakori' is a book that will keep you engrossed throughout. The events leading to the daring plot by the revolutionaries is narrated very nicely. It virtually takes you to the period and shows the state of mind of the youth at that time. The struggles of these revolutionaries, the agony and torture faced by them and their families. In spite of this, how they managed to finish the task is written beautifully. The language is simple and lucid. Smitaji has been doing research on the subject for quite some time now and had mentioned about her intention to write about it when we met at a Lucknow event 2 years ago. I thank Smitaji for writing such a wonderful book and thus highlighting the invaluable contribution of many such unsung heroes who have not received their deserved recognition in the freedom struggle of India.

– **Chetanji Chaphekar**
Nasik, Maharashtra

By Satyasheel Ji Rajguru (Shaheed ShivramJi Hari Rajguru's grandson)

An imaginary storyline woven around a daring piece of our Indian freedom struggle – The Kakori Conspiracy. The conspiracy of armed robbery of the train from Kakori to plunder funds from the British Treasury for revolutionary actions against the British atrocities. It was organised by the Hindustan Republican Association (HRA), under Shri Ram Prasad Bismilji, supported by Ashfaqulla Khanji, Thakur Roshanji, Rajendra Lahiriji, and many more heroes. They were later tried and sentenced to death. Many others were sent to kalapani.

Mrs. Smitaji Dhruv has presented the act and the events that followed in a very gripping way. The tortuous acts upon the martyrs and their families that followed have been presented and the selfless sacrifice and actions of our heroes for our freedom acknowledged.

My grandfather Shaheed Shivram Hari Rajguru, came from a far corner of Maharashtra, all fired up to lay down his life for the freedom of his motherland. There were thousands of martyrs who came from all corners of the country — young men, ladies and children. It is very important that such books are written and read so that the untold acts of heroic sacrifice, inspire love and respect for all our countrymen irrespective of caste, creed, religion and gender. It will teach us to value our freedom above all.

I heartily congratulate Smitaji, for her successful efforts in this direction, and specially recommend the youth to buy and read this book. I also wish her all the best on her future accomplishments.

– **Mr. Satyasheel Kamalakar Rajguru**

Pune

By Rajendra Nath Ji Bakshi (Shachindra Nath Ji Bakshi's son)

Shachindranath Ji Bakshi **Rajendranath Ji Bakshi**

It is very commendable that Mrs. Smita Dhruv is inspired deeply by the martyrs and revolutionaries of India, who gave up their lives and everything to free India from the British yoke, that she decided to bring the names and dedication of these martyrs and revolutionaries By publishing a book 'Destination Kakori; 9th August, 1925', so that the present generation can know about their dedication, which can inspire the young generation for the welfare of our society and the nation. I hope, she will continue to write and publish these types of books which inspire the people of today's India.

– **Rajendranath Ji Bakshi**

51/1, Tikait Rai LDA Colony,

Lucknow - 226017 U.P.

❑

Author's Note & Acknowledgements

अपि स्वर्णमयी लंका न मे लक्ष्मण रोचते।
जननी जन्मभूमिश्च स्वर्गादपि गरीयसी।।

'Lakshman, even this golden Lanka does not appeal to me. Mother and motherland are superior even to heaven.'

This is from the Indian Epic, Ramayan in which Shri Ram tells his younger brother Laxman, as they return from the gold-laden Lanka.

Many of India's freedom fighters believed in the ideology of this Verse (shlok), who fought for India's freedom. I too humbly believe in it as well.

Whenever I saw the pictures of the Indian freedom struggle, depicting Indians fighting the British forces, I used to wonder, 'Who are all the hundreds and thousands of people other than faces of the known leaders - to die by a gun-shot or sent to the gallows or tortured in the cellular jails?

There has to be a mention of them, hidden somewhere in the archives of the blood-soaked history. After all, India's journey for its freedom against the British rulers was not entirely out of non- violence or a peaceful process, as it is made to appear.

It is written on the East Gallery of the wall of Berlin and how aptly this applies to our country's freedom fighters!

'Many small people who in many small places do many small things that can alter the face of the world.'

There is a plethora of information on India's freedom struggle and about many famous leaders, their patriotism and devotion towards the fight against the British Government.

But as Napolean Bonaparte himself had quoted,

'History is the version of past events that people have decided to agree upon.'

The freedom of our country has neither been gained overnight, nor has it been possible by efforts of a handful of leaders. Unfortunately, what remains today is merely the version that history books have propagated and people have accepted.

And thus, my search began by diving into the unknown stories of the unsung heroes in the unknown history books.

While going through the India's freedom history, I often came across 'Magna Carta' or 'Queen's Proclamation' or 'Rowlatt Act' time and again and I wondered why these events were so important for us to know?

Do we know about ....

- Vasudeo Balwant Phadke? 'Shivaji of the freedom struggle?'
- The fearless gatha of the great Chaphekar Bandhus?
- About Barrister Vir Savarkar who was tied to the oil extracting unit, in place of an ox (Kolhu ka Bail) every morning at the Cellular jails?
- How Chandrashekhar Azad took beatings at the court at the young age of 15 years? Mahavir Singh was forced to take milk while fasting by a tube which punctured his lungs in the jail, causing his death?
- That Bhagat Singh fasted for 163 days, before he went to gallows?
- Ram Prasad Bismil used to starve for days since his team-mates could not afford to buy food?
- Shachindranath Bakshi's memoirs where he has mentioned about how he cleverly trapped a British CID agent?
- Salim Garh Fort, where Indian National Army soldiers were jailed and tortured (after their unsuccessful attempt to free India under the leadership of SubhashBabu), lies in the Red Fort campus itself? It is said that even today cries of the soldiers undergoing tortures are heard in the silent nights in New Delhi.

We must know this important history, because it is the sacrifices of these heroes that has won India its freedom!

While reading these lesser known stories, I embarked upon an incident, a brave, head-on conspiracy by the *Krantiveers* against the British which has gone unnoticed in the India's history by the political leaders and Indian masses. It was the 'Kakori Conspiracy' that took place on the 9th August, 1925 by a few unsung heroes which shook the pillars of the British empire in India for the first time.

It goes back to the timeline of 1919, by the end of which, there was a widespread political discontent against the British Government in India. The Jallianwala Bagh massacre by General Dyre culminated in the Non-Cooperation Movement under Gandhiji's leadership. This was the first mass based political movement after the mutiny of 1857.

The Non-Cooperation Movement was launched on 1st August 1920. It had a tremendous effect on the masses of India. There was a clear protest where people would refuse to buy British goods. They would rather adopt the use of local handicrafts, picket liquor shops, take out processions and organise meetings. Students had left schools and colleges, and were ready to fight back! The fire of this collective non-cooperation had spread all over India!

Unity in the country was strengthened and many Indian schools and colleges were established. Indian goods were being encouraged to be purchased.

The long standing grievances of the toiling masses against the British, as well as the Indian masters got an opportunity through this movement to express their real feelings.

The success of the revolt was a total shock to British autorities and a massive encouragement to millions of Indian nationalists.

Sadly, the Non-Cooperation Movement was abruptly withdrawn and that too very soon on 10th March 1922, the reasons remained unexplained.

As a result, hundreds and thousands of people who had joined this movement — majority of which was the youth of India — were disillusioned and disappointed.

Death of this movement created an upheaval in the minds of those involved, and this deceit saw birth of a large number of revolutionaries.

The revolutionary groups believed in armed revolution against the ruling British, and were mainly concentrated in Bengal, Maharashtra, Bihar, the United Provinces (Uttar Pradesh and Uttarakhand) and Punjab. There were number of smaller groups, which were scattered across India.

These unsung heroes rose on various occasions, to fight against the British rule, eventually to be crushed by its powerful forces.

During their fight, they lived under the most horrifying circumstances — away from their families, often imprisoned, to be tortured to die, and many of them climbing the gallows one after the other! Soon they faded away from the pages of history – leaving no signs of their existence in the chapters of India's freedom struggle! Thus, their stories remained unknown to the people of India forever!

All this information and pathos of it pushed my dream project 'Destination Kakori: 9th August, 1925' into reality.

It is a fictional story of the times when Non-Cooperation Movement had failed. My inspiration in writing a historical fictioncame from the legendary late Shri Kanaiyalal Munshi Ji, the founder of Bhavan's colleges, a lawyer and a proficient Gujarati author.

Thus began my journey.

I started writing the story, sometimes expeditiously and at times taking a back seat completely.

A story of Mukund Pandey and Satish Gupta, Banvari Gupta, Leela (Gupta) Pandey, Birendra Sharma, and their contemporaries, whose lives were sacrificed for one such mission named 'Kakori Train Robbery'.

The story starts with a narration by Mukund, a dedicated follower of the British, a student, who later became an employee of the Indian Railways. The narrative of the story is picked up by other characters eventually.

His close friend, Satish (*Bagga*), joins one of the revolutionary groups. His elder brother Banvari is already working on this mission for some time.

Satish and Banvari are a family of two brothers and three sisters, and their parents, where two of the elder sisters were victimised by hazards of dowry and subsequent tortures from in-laws.

Leela is the only surviving sister, who marries Mukund eventually.

Banvari, Satish and Birendra (their nephew who is survived after his mother's death) get engulfed by the fire of freedom struggle for India.

Each person narrates to unfold the story and carry it further.

One of the narrations is by Mr.Kirstein, a British Railway officer who is Mukund's boss, arriving from London for a special Railway assignment in India.

His narration provides a different perspective to the process of colonisation in India.

This historical fiction depicts deep mental agony of people of India in those times, their dilemma and survival issues at every stage.

The facts about the Kakori Train Robbery, which took place on 9th August, 1925 is the concluding event.

Many coincidences took place during the writing of this book, about which I happened to learn later.

In my story, the nick-name of the freedom fighter Satish was 'Bagga', that was in fact the nick-name of none other than shaheed-e-azam Bhagat Singh Ji!

Again, in the story, Satish's best friend is Mukund, his elder brother's classmate. In reality, Ram Prasad Bismil was classmate of Ashfaq Ulla Khan Ji's elder brother!

I also consider it a miracle to find 'After five years in India' a book written by Anne C. Wilson, wife of a Deputy Commissioner, Magistrate and collector in 1895, in Calcutta which depicted the lives of the British citizens in India and how they saw India through their eyes.

I have taken the liberty to weave an imaginary story out of experiences of revolutionaries as follows;

1. Manmathnath Ji Gupta (from his book 'They lived Dangerously' English; ManmathNath Gupta, People's publishing House & Hind Pocket Books, New Delhi, 1971).
2. Shachindranath Ji Bakshi ('Kranti ke path par – Ek Krantikari ke sansmaran' Hindi, By Shachindra Nath Bakshi, Lokhit Prakashan, Lucknow, 2006).
3. Ramprasad Ji Bismil, and his sister ('Amar Krantkari Ramprasad Bismil ki Atmakatha 'Hindi, By Pandit Satyanarayan Sharma, Sakshi Prakashan, New Delhi, 2013)
4. Information about Indian Railways

'http://www.gktoday.in/blog/acworth-committee-on-indian- railways/to facilitate the reader take a peep into the real lives of these legends.

I am indebted to all of them, and must confess that I could bring life into the story with the help of these invaluable books.

While visiting Lucknow several times, the vibe of the city and its people have always inspired me to write more about India's freedom struggle! One of them was the event that took place in December 2017 to felicitate the descendents of our freedom fighters.

This event had helped me to meet luminaries like Shri Shaileshji Tilak (Grandson of Lokmanyaji Tilak), Shri Chetanji Chaphekar (from the great Chaphekarji family), Ashfaq Ulla Khanji (from the

Ashfaq Ulla Khanji family), Shri Jagmohan Singhji (from BhagatSinghji's family), Shri Udayji Khatri (descendent of the Ramkrishnaji Khatri) and many more.

I consider myself fortunate as *Shri Chetanji* (descendent of Chapekarji Bandhus), *Shri SatyashilJi* (Grandson of Shivramji Hari Rajguru), *Shri Rajendra Nathji Bakshi* (descendent of Shachindra Nathji Bakshi) have kindly blessed by writing reviews for the book, without which 'Destination Kakori: 9th August, 1925' would have been incomplete

I have been given invaluable support, in the form of constant encouragement provided by my daughters Kanan and Kelly, to bring my book to completion. My husband Amal was always enthusiastic to send me to remotest places like Kakori, Salim Garh Fort, visit Lucknow several times, and often accompanied me too!

I am thankful to the Times of India group for allowing me to use their archives, and providing me with a copy of the required information.

I am thankful to my dear friends for their appreciation and motivation.

I am thankful to Mr.Sharma, a retired Station Master of Lucknow, whose help by sending 'Autobiography of Ramprasad Bismil' pushed me to kick-start this book's journey. Chandrakant Maurya, our Bhaiyaji's son, helped source many such books to me from Lucknow.

Today, as I present 'Destination Kakori: 9th August, 1925' to my स्वगाणिदि गरीयसी country and to the world, I seek blessings from the soul and soil of India and its great heritage, culture and ethos which stretches over hundreds of centuries. I sincerely hope that my attempt to highlight a small episode from the precious Indian freedom struggle will be appreciated by all the readers and memories of these martyrs will come alive in their hearts after 70 years of freedom!

JAI HIND

Content

Non-Cooperation Movement called off

Mukund Narrates

I turned in disbelief towards Birendra, a young boy in his teens with an innocent face, and good features inherited from his mother.

'Did Satish ask me to come instantly? Why did he sound so worried?'

Birendra could not understand my question. He waited eagerly for either a reply or an instant action from me.

I remember the day vividly.

It was 18th of March, 1922.

I was enjoying the cool morning breeze sitting on the steps of the front courtyard of my house, in Muzeim Nagar Lucknow, when Birendra came rushing towards me.

'Uncle Mukund! Mohandas Gandhi has called off the Non-Cooperation Movement and he might be arrested again! Satish Uncle has called you home urgently!'

Though the distant communication was a rarity in those days, some news used to spread at a lightning speed. In this case, the credit went to Birendra, of course.

He used to live with his maternal grandparents after his mother passed away. He was the nephew of my friend, Satish.

Birendra most often worked as a messenger between Satish and myself, but today the situation sounded very unusual.

Satish would never be disturbed by any news pertaining to India's freedom struggle nor did it ever interest me.

Besides, it was only yesterday that we had met at the college, when Satish had brought me a job application form, for a job at the Indian Railways, as I was completing my Graduation in Arts this year. Satish had still two more years to complete his Graduation.

However, it was futile to ask anything from Birendra. I decided to know it from Satish himself.

'Let me find out what is wrong with Satish', I mumbled and got up.

I got up with many questions storming my mind, put on my chappals and in the same pyjama- kurta rushed to Satish's house.

In fact, even if given an opportunity, I could hardly boast of better clothes to change into.

Young Birendra was happy to see me coming along and followed me excitedly.

Ramnagar, where Satish lived, was one of the elite areas of Lucknow.It was not very far from my house in Muzeim Nagar.

I lived in a small house, just adequate for our small family, being the only son of a British fearing father and a mother suffering with many chronic ailments.

We soon reached Ramnagar, the area with many big houses.

They were built in a specific pattern. Each house had a sprawling courtyard, sprawling backyards and architecture of a unique design and architecture.

The approach road was too dusty as usual. In fact, it was not a defined road where one could walk with ease.

There were neem, peepal and bargad trees spread out on both the sides giving the place an appearance of a small jungle. The road was rutted with the wheels of the bullock carts and the tongas rarely passed by.

Few farmers could be seen at the horizon with their bullocks going towards their farms, it being the morning time.

We reached the last big house in the first lane in about fifteen minutes. That was Satish's house. Satish, Banvari and Leela's house.

I had always admired this house. Anyone could be envious of the people who owned such a massive and royal house!

The doors of the grand house were of solid timber, with carvings at the top edge and the corners.

The house had large chiselled windows with colourful glasses adding grandeur to them. An extensive porch spoke volumes about the prosperity it possessed in the recent past.

I knocked on the large carved teakwood door and, in a few moments, it creaked opened to expose the exquisite interior of the beautiful house.

As the door opened, the high ceiling and vastness of the place were apparent automatically.

A tall woman in her late forties opened the door, with her head covered with the pallu of a red and yellow floral saree.

Though she had worn scanty ornaments, her royal demeanour could not be concealed. She was beautiful, but had intentionally tried to hide her beauty to appear older than her age.

As a paradox, her eyes spoke of a fear that could not be extinguished. Perhaps, this was the result of being in a family which had been living jointly for many generations under the same roof.

I bowed respectfully to Kamala Chachi, Satish's mother.

Seeing me at the door, her eyes gleamed with some relief, as she exclaimed, 'Mukund, You have come at the right time! Something is wrong with your friend today!'

I could sense anxiety in her voice. I asked, 'What happened? Where is Bagga?'

'Bagga' was Satish's nick-name by which his close family and friends addressed him.

She pointed towards the back of the house and said with concern in her tone, 'He is pacing up and down restlessly in the backyard.'

Kamala Chachi was like a second mother to me. I could talk toher for hours. She could have narrated the situation in a normal manner, had I asked her about Bagga's restlessness, but that wouldn't have been appropriate today. Today there was a trouble brewing in the air.

Refraining myself from talking to her, I hurriedly entered the house.

I entered the large central hall, which was connected to other rooms and led to a narrow passage that curved little further to reach the backyard.

Satish's great- grandfather, Bansilal had built this house.

In fact, he had received many recognitions and rewards from the Government for his business acumen and the charitable works for the society about seventy years ago.

The land on which this house was built, was one of them.

That explained the creation of the beautiful house, done with great taste and extravagancy.

While entering the backyard, I observed that the spring had evidently settled in. After the fall (autumn) season, which had just got over, the trees were adorned with new, fresh and plush green leaves.

The architecture of the backyard and its small garden was very eye- catching.

> *Tall and sprawling neem, mango, banyan and asopalav trees grew in abundance. Vacant spaces were filled with the plants laden with colourful flowers such as bougainvillea, sunflower, marigold etc. spread all around making the whole place appear like a heaven of colours.*

I tried to turn my gaze away from the beauty of the place and started looking for Satish.

Satish was a tall and fair complexioned young boy with piercing eyes. He paced the backyard with long strides. His strong physique reminded one of an athlete, who seemed very agitated presently.

Satish was not always like this. In fact, Satish that I knew during the college times was usually a calm person, with a cool temperament, laughing and joking around with his friends. He regularly participated in debates, sports competitions, and in almost all the extra-curricular activities held in the college. This had made him very popular among friends. He was a born leader which he proved in the very first year of the college.

Of course, he had very strong views on certain issues like the system of law and freedom of our country which I learnt after spending some more time with him.

But today his disposition and body language gave the impression of a trapped lion eager to jump out from the cage.

I was clueless. Something was disturbing him greatly. There was a massive banyan tree in centre of the backyard.

A stone seat was built under it. This was my favourite place where I loved to sit whenever I visited Satish's house.

I entered the backyard and sat there waiting impatiently.

Satish was pacing aggressively up and down in the free space, between the seat and the light swing, which was placed on other side of the huge tree.

Banvari was there too, sitting on the bench. Unlike Satish, he appeared calm.

In fact, this was how Banvari always looked, inconspicuous and unimpressive, so much so one might often tend to ignore him.

Whenever I had an opportunity to interact with Banvari, he spoke in short sentences, and few words. He was never interested in studies though, and looked preoccupied all the time.

Even while participating in the college activites, he was indifferent and disinterested unlike Satish.

Satish, Banvari and myself studied together at the *Lucknow University College*. Banvari was in my batch, but our acquaintance could never turn into friendship, the way it was between Satish and me. While walking together to the college and returning home, we had become close friends.

Sometimes Satish took my help for solving difficulties regarding studies. I was good at Economics and English, and used to top the class as a rule. The professors in the college, Indian as well as foreigners, always involved me in the class discussions and the debates.

As a result, many of my co-students and juniors liked to discuss difficulties regarding studies with me. Satish being a bright student himself, used to discuss not only studies but all the topics under the sun.

This friendship often brought me to his house. But today it was a different matter altogether.

As soon as Satish saw me, he turned and stopped.

In one leap, he came towards me, held my hand and gave vent to his agitation and restlessness. 'Aa gaya tu Mukund? Nayi khabar tu ne suni kya?' (So, you are here Mukund! Did you hear the latest news?)

I was surprised. Did he mean news about the freedom struggle?

However, I wanted to know more. My curiosity was growing.

Satish sat next to me on the ground and continued with his outburst, 'Was that a correct decision to call off the Non-Cooperation Movement?' This left me dumbfounded.

What was wrong with Satish? Why was he speaking like his brother Banvari, who never let go any opportunity to speak critically against the leaders of India's freedom struggle?

Why should anyone be affected by the freedom struggle and its issues so intensely?

While coming to Satish's house, I had been thinking on the way that Satish might be facing difficulties in Economics or Mathematics, or there was some gossip about the University, that he wanted to share with me.

I was disappointed. He had called me to discuss India's freedom struggle.

I tried to remind him about our discussion which we had while returning from the college yesterday.

'Bagga! Remember what had happened at Chauri-Chaura? That was a negative reaction to the Non-Cooperation Movement. In such grave situations the citizens of the country shouldn't take law in their hands.'

On that day, our discussion had stopped at that juncture.

I had tried to divert his mind saying that the exams were approaching fast, and it was important for everyone to study and pass with good marks.

But today Satish had the support of his elder brother Banvari who intervened.

'I completely disagree with you, Mukund. The news is circulated that the protesters attacked the police and burnt them alive. However, this is only half the truth, and one side of the story.'

'In reality, a peaceful procession shouting the usual slogans was passing by a police station. The police present there started firing at the procession, consequently a lot of protesters were injured and succumbed to the firing. The protesters were immensely enraged. Out of frenzy, the otherwise peaceful group turned into a hostile mob and chased the policemen to the police station and set fire to it.'

As Banvari was describing the incident at Chauri-Chaura, his voice was trembling with grief and emotions.

He coughed a little to continue, "And as a result, the Non- Cooperation movement was suspended!"

Satish was agitated, "How can anyone decide this without consulting the people of India? The sanctity of the freedom struggle is lost now. We have lost a great opportunity for acquiring freeom for our country!"

"Mukund, do you remember when we went to Jallianwala Baag?"

He started to pace up and down again. "Wo shahadat har raat meri nazron ke samne chha jati hai" (that martyrdom comes alive before my eyes every night).

He added, "It haunts me. I ought to do something now." I remembered that incident very vividly.

We had gone to Amritsar on a weekend a few months ago. Some of the students from our college had organised the trip and it was then that we had visited Jallianwala Bagh.

Only three years back, to be exact, on Sunday, 13th April, 1919, there was a simple meeting in the Bagh, where the people of Amritsar had gathered to celebrate the festival of Baisakhi.

The Jallianwala Bagh is an assembly chowk surrounded by buildings on all the sides. It has a narrow passage to go inside, and unfortunately, that serves as the exit too.

Brigadier General Dyer was posted there by the Jalandhar Cantonment some time back. He was somehow convinced that a major revolt was to take place, so he had banned all the meetings. However, this notice was not widely circulated.

On hearing that a gathering had assembled at the Jallianwala Bagh, Dyer went there with hundreds of soldiers and ordered them to open fire on the unarmed citizens. Dyer continued the firing until the ammunition supply was almost exhausted and as a result thousands of innocent people died in the cold-blooded killing.

That place till date resounds with the piercing cries of the unbearable pain and apprehension which rose amid the brutal massacre, where no one, old men, women or children, no one was spared. The haunting eerieness of the place spoke of merciless killings of more than a thousand people who gathered there just to meet and exchange Baisakhi greetings with each other.

There were innumerable holes made on the walls by the bullets fired from the British soldiers' rifles. The blood was splashed on the walls and on the ground, everywhere.

We reached there. Satish stood still for a long time and kept staring at the ground motionless, without uttering a word.

It must have been almost half an hour, when I went near him and shook him. "Bagga, what happened? Are you okay?"

All the friends gathered around him, and tried to pacify him, but he stood still and motionless. He appeared shaken to roots. Then suddenly, he picked up some soil from the ground in his palm, folded it in his handkerchief and put it in his pocket. None of us could understand what had happened to him. He said, " I have kept the soil I had brought from the Jallianwala Bagh in front of my bed, so that every morning when I wake up, I can see it."

I was surprised. He had never mentioned about it before.

Admittedly, I was disturbed by the painful experience too, but I had accepted this as a mistake committed by the Government in enforcing discipline and law and order in the country.

'The Rulers know the best' is what I had argued with myself, and let it pass out of my memory.

The mention of the Jallianwala Bagh massacre irritated me in this situation. Why open the closed chapters now?

I did not want Satish to be carried away by such rebellious thoughts.

"Bagga! Rahene de, Dost! (Bagga, leave it, my friend!) There are already thousands of people fighting for this cause. Besides, the King Emperor's army is very powerful. We are too weak and small to fight against them."

But it hardly seemed to have any effect on Satish.

He did not find it to be a valid excuse and said, "That is why I am certain that one has to die for the country, if it has to be freed from the foreigners. Either you be ready to sacrifice your life, or stay as a slave under their rule."

Banvari joined in.

'Non-Cooperation Movement was a brilliant idea through which the people of India had united for the freedom struggle. But why should it be called off so suddenly?'

Banvari seemed to have a different agenda on his mind. Everyone knew that he was associated with a revolutionary group in the city.

Satish argued, "The leaders should have thought about its consequences and the repercussions before declaring this movement. They had promised a free nation within one year. Who will believe them now?"

Frankly, I found all the arguments meaningless and wastage of the time, as far as our future was concerned, it was based on studies. Our exams were fast approaching and that is what mattered in the present scenario.

After a few moments' silence Satish declared, 'Mukund, Gandhi might have given up, but I am not giving up my fight.'

I looked at him in bewilderment.

His eyes had a different glint in them now, like a fanatic's. It was sad to see the bitterly aggressive side of a cheerful person like Satish who was immensely loved by all the friends and family.

While Satish was speaking, Banvari was listening to him intently. It was apparent that both the brothers were beginning to think alike now. Satish's thoughts were completely influenced by that of Banvari's.

I began to recall the happy days spent with Bagga in the college.

Though he was my junior, Satish was an uncrowned leader of the students. He could spontaneously paint a doodle of any professor on the blackboard or tie a donkey to the bicycle of a friend! He was known for his practical but harmless pranks and jokes which he played all the time to bring smiles on his friends' faces. At the same time, he was dependable and helpful in the times of crisis.

However, under the funny exterior of Bagga, there was hidden a strong willed and dedicated patriot, embodying an inherent volcano of resentment and revolt against the Raj, which could erupt anytime.

By the time the Non-Cooperation Movement was announced, Satish was a regular student at the college who participated in various activities and was also good at studies.

In fact, when some of the college students had planned to organise protests against the Government to support the Non-Cooperation Movement, Satish was reluctant to join the same.

Obviously, I too had discouraged him as I was under the complete influence of my father and considered myself responsible for my parents' happy and safe future.

I had always seen my father laugh at any news published in the newspapers about the fight for freedom and the protests. He believed that nothing would come out of all this.

If anyone mentioned to my father about the tasks and the efforts carried out by great leaders like Gandhi, Lala Lajpatrai, Motilal Nehru or Subhash Chandra Bose, he would shake his head and say, "These movements will never be successful. Everyone wants to become a leader. No one thinks about the collective good of our country. Instead, it would be wiser to listen to the King Emperor's men, who are here to discipline our people and modernise the country."

It was obvious that my thoughts spoke of my father's beliefs.

My chain of thoughts was broken when Satish's sister Leela, their youngest sibling, entered the backyard carrying tea for us.

Leela was a lively girl and she would often participate in our discussions but today she did not join the conversation.

She placed the tray near Banvari and returned quickly.

Sipping the aromatic masala tea in an earthen cup, I tried to divert the topic, "Banvari, how are your preparations for the exams going on?"

Banvari did not respond to my question. Instead, he continued sipping his tea, lost in some thoughts. After a few moments, he replied quietly, "Mukund, I am more concerned about the state of things in our country now."

Satish nodded in agreement with Banvari.

It was clear that both the brothers were indifferent towards the college exams, or anything else except their concern for the country.

Banvari was never in awe of the education system established by the British, and moreover now Satish had changed his mind on this issue as well. I felt that to both Banvari and Satish all this conversation was meaningless. Looking at Satish and Banvari's aggression on the Non-Cooperation Movement issue, I realised that I was wasting my time, any argument with them was now futile.

For me, on the other hand, passing the final college exam was very important. It was my life, my future, my aspirations and promises to my parents - it was everything!

With a short and quick reply, "Okay, Bagga, you can do as you wish. I have to go back home to help mother." I left Satish and Banvari to themselves, and got up to leave.

However, Satish's words kept ringing in my ears. The conversation with him and Banvari had taken complete charge of my thoughts.

I was terrified to learn about my friend's thinking about the political developments in the country. At no cost did I want to compromise on the priorities of my life and join him and Banvari in this mission!

Exasperated by the turn of events, I went and stood near the window in my small room.

This was in fact my parents' bedroom, the only bedroom in our house, where I liked to sit and study.

There was an old cot which was little broader than a single bed, and a chair and a table in the room. The old furniture which was preserved year after year. The entire household was managed somehow with my father's meagre earnings.

He was an ordinary clerk. He had taken many years to reach the second level of seniority in the Registry office of the Government. This was a big leap for our family. Prior to father getting this job, our family business was to perform rituals (poojas) during the religious and the auspicious days.

Of course, it was not my family background or the past that mattered to me today, but it was my friendship with Satish, which was at stake and a matter of real concern for me.

Some old memories of the good old times, when I had met Satish for the first time at the University, came rushing to my mind in torrents.

It was beginning of the new academic year (my third and final year). I would be securing the Bachelor of Arts degree at the end of this year.

I had reached college a little early on the first day of the new academic year. Undoubtedly, I was very happy and excited to resume my college studies, after scoring a higher second class in my last exam.

Lucknow University had a huge building and a sprawling campus.

The main college building was led by a long path from the central gate, and vastness of the building added to the awe that the students experienced as soon as they entered the campus.

It was an undisputed fact that our university was acclaimed to be very prestigious.

It began under the supervision and advise of the great Sir Michael Sadler who was the founder of the Sadler Commision. He was an adviser to the Viceroy Lord Chelmsford, and had come to Hindustan to study and prepare report on the education system of our country.

It was recently established by converting the Canning College as a part of the University and some new colleges were built in the process.

In a short span, Lucknow University had grown very popular. There were many more students enrolling for various degrees in the college every year.

We were fortunate to have professors like Prof. Radha Kamal Mukherjee for Economics, Dr. Bazl-ur-Rahman for Literature in Persian language and many more prominent professors for all the departments imparting education in various subjects.

The Department of English literature was headed by the British professors.

There was a galaxy of good professors who were invited from various parts of the country and abroad at regular intervals.

My father was the happiest person when I had secured admission in this college, and he was certain that I will make him proud one day, and hopefully will work for the government on a high post.

Nonetheless, that day I was standing at the main gate watching the hustle and bustle of the first-year students from the front stairs, with typical air of a senior who looks down at the juniors.

The students had started trickling in from the main gate.

Many had nervously entered the college, whereas some were still standing at the entrance not knowing what to do.

Interestingly, one boy was neither looking nervous nor confused, just naturally curious to be in a new place.

He appeared familiar to me. As I went closer, I could immediately recognise him. He was Satish, Banvari's brother.

I asked him, "You are Satish, right? Banvari's younger brother?"

Satish smiled at me and said, "Namaste Bhaiya! Khub pehchana aapne."

(Hello Brother! You are absolutely right!)

I had taken an instant liking for this tall, well built, confident boy.

I introduced myself, 'Satish, I am Mukund, Banvari's friend and Pandey Ji's son, who works with your father.'

He joined his hands in a namaste gesture.

'Yes, Mukund Bhaiya, I know. The Registry department of the High Court.' Satish smiled, and I smiled in return.

However, Satish and Banvari's father was at a higher rank in the office, compared to my father, who was a simple clerk and had been serving at that level for many years.

I was happy to notice that this fact had not changed Satish's behaviour towards me. This attracted me towards him instantly.

After the college, we again ran into each other. We were pleasantly surprised to know that we didn't live too far from each other, and decided to return home together, which eventually became a routine for both of us.

While walking back from the college, we used to share a lot of ideas, and our future plans. Why was I slipping into the past again? I tried to control myself.

'Enough of thinking about the past' I told myself. I opened the window for some fresh air.

A cool and fresh breeze blew into the room, which was helpful in disassociating myself from the impact of conversation with Satish and Banvari, to some extent.

I did not realise that almost two hours had passed in this state, the evening shadows were gradually turning into the night. I had to get back to study as soon as possible.

After finishing my dinner quickly, I took out a textbook, and made a futile attempt to read.

As the time passed, the disturbance returned with all the more vengeance, and I could not decide whether to sleep or study. In the end, I yielded to an easier option and went off to sleep.

As the new day began, I laughed off everything that had happened at Satish's house the previous day.

My assumption was that Satish will get back to his studies, if not Banvari, and take the political happenings in his stride.

No sooner did this thought cross my mind, then I was greatly relieved and started studying with full attention.

Should I say that I was trying to ignore Satish for the next few days?

It was already past ten days since our last meeting. Since I had not heard from Bagga till now, I decided to catch the two brothers at the college. Satish had a habit of visiting the college in the morning hours, and catch up with his studies and deliver references as well.

When I reached the college, much to my dismay, I could neither find Satish nor Banvari anywhere. I looked around in all the likely places in the college - classrooms, corridors, and the college compound.

Suddenly I recalled that Satish often visited the college library. It was a little away from the regular classrooms.

As I reached there, I stood aghast! Something unbelievable seemed to have happened there. The library doors were closed and sealed.

Horrified, I ran closer to the library door. There was a notice which read:

'Permission is withdrawn to access this area.' It was signed by the Commisioner of Police, Lucknow.

This did not explain anything. On the contrary, it confused and scared me.

I sat down on a bench there.

I hoped and prayed that this had nothing to do with Satish and Banvari's discussion with me that evening. A strange frustration and apprehension surrounded me. I desparately looked here and there to find some answer.

Satish Narrates

I still recall the day when all this had started.

I was appearing for my final exams of the penultimate year of school with the last two papers still remaining.

On 6th April, 1919 Mohandas Karamchand Gandhi announced a nationwide Satyagraha against the Rowlett act.

People were certain that this movement will bring freedom for Hindustan soon.

It was a new thought, as refreshing as the freedom itself.

Ironically, after only four days of Gandhi's decision, on 10th April, the police opened fire on a procession in Amritsar and the Martial law was imposed.

This was followed by the black day, 13th April, 1919 in the history of the British rule in India.

The heart-rending inhuman massacre of thousands of innocent people curdled everyone's blood. It included women and children as well. The earth was drenched in blood at the Jallianwala Bagh in Amritsar by General Dyer.

People were stunned. The hidden killer tendency of the ruler's men was exposed. The whole nation awoke from the deep slumber. Leaders of the colonised India, who were fighting for the independence were horrified.

When I heard about this from Banvari Bhaiya (my elder brother), I was very desparate to join the freedom movement like many of my school friends.

However, when I told Bhaiya about my decision, he refused right away and said that this was not the right time for me to join the movement. He felt I was too young for it. Instead, I must focus on my studies and complete my graduation.

Little did I know that Banvari Bhaiya used to attend all the secret meetings and often participated in the processions which were organised in Lucknow.

It took me two years to complete my schooling successfully. I joined the Lucknow University for degree in Arts.

My parents, my younger sister Leela and especially Banvari Bhaiya were very happy.

Since the thought of joining the freedom struggle was temporarily dropped, I could properly focus on my studies at the college.

During this time, I had become friendly with Mukund, who was in fact two years elder to me. He was from a family very well-known to my father, and quite good in studies.

It was my first year at the college, and he influenced me greatly to study well.

Soon we had become good friends. I admired his dedication for studies.

At the time of the quarterly and mid-term exams, he would patiently solve my difficulties, especially things such as concept of Economics or a poem in English literature.

Our friendship grew stronger mainly because we returned together from the college, almost everyday. On our way back home, we discussed every topic under the sun. Together we had also decided to apply for the Government jobs, hence both of us used to work out various job applications.

Then came the Non-Cooperation Movement, which was launched on 1st August, 1920.

In January 1921, this movement picked up pace. Its echoes had begun to resound not only in the big cities, but also in the remote villages in the country.

The reports said that Gandhi had lost all the faith in the goodness of the British Government and declared that it would be a 'sin' to cooperate with the 'Satanic' Government.

In his Non-Cooperation Movement against the British Raj, this time Gandhi appealed to the youth of India to give up modes of violence against the Government for a year, at the end of which he promised to free their mother land.

The movement was to be nonviolent and to consist of Indians resigning their titles; boycotting government educational institutions, the courts, government services, foreign goods, and elections and eventually refusing to pay taxes.

Non-Cooperation was agreed to, by the Indian National Congress at Calcutta (now Kolkata) in September 1920 and was launched that December.

In 1921 the government, confronted with united Indian front for the first time, was visibly shaken, but a revolt by the Muslim Moplahs of Kerala (southwestern India) in August 1921 and a number of violent outbreaks alarmed moderate opinion.

Everyone believed in Gandhi and the impact was very strong this time. The people of India were ready to sacrifice everything for the freedom of their country.

As a result, the students left their schools and colleges and hundreds of young men left their homes. The lawyers gave up their practices and people resigned from their jobs. They all had faith that Gandhi will create a miracle!

[The eminent Hindi writer, poet, play-wright, journalist and nationalist Rambriksh Benipuri, who spent more than eight years in prison fighting for India's independence, wrote: 'When I recall Non-Cooperation era of 1921, the image of a storm confronts my eyes. From the time I became aware, I have witnessed numerous movements, however, I can assert that no other movement upturned the foundations of Indian society to the extent that the Non-Cooperation Movement did. From the humblest huts to the high places, from villages to cities, everywhere there was a ferment, a loud echo.']

Unfortunately, a shocking disaster took place and the hell broke loose. I couldn't believe my ears when I heard the news that Gandhi is calling off the Non-Cooperation Movement.

As a result, hundreds and thousands of Hindustanis were disillusioned.

Many said that there was unrest among the leaders too.

The step taken by Gandhi did not receive the approval of any of the Congress leaders. C.R. Das, Motilal Nehru, Jawaharlal Nehru, who were in the prison condemned it strongly.

Nobody had an answer to Gandhi's decision for calling off the movement.

Unfortunately, none of the leaders fighting for the freedom of India, tried to meet or reach to the masses in such a crucial moment.

People looked completely dismayed and disoriented as they waited for the leaders to speak up and discuss the next plan of action to show them the right way.

Banvari Bhaiya was already in disagreement with the calling off of the Non-Cooperation Movement, and I was certain that he would take up this as an important mission of his life.

Mukund's strong influence and Banvari Bhaiya's command prevented me from participating in the fight for the freedom.

The college exams were approaching soon. I wanted Mukund to guide me whether to drop out and skip the annual exams this term.

I sent Biru to call Mukund, and he did come running like a true friend.

I told him about the state of concern our country was going through and how serious the things were, but it had no effect whatsoever on him.

Mukund's only concern was his final B.A. exams that would take place in a month's time. He was solely occupied by the motive of completing his studies and securing a job in a government company.

This disappointed me greatly.

I didn't agree with his ideology! If we did not participate in the fight today for the great purpose, perhaps it would be too late then.

For the first time I felt annoyed towards him. He turned out to be one of those who cared only for his own future, and sleep peacefully at night by mortgaging his self- esteem to the gora log (Britishers).

All this time I hopefully depended upon Mukund for him to find some way out for his distraught friend. But he proved me wrong. On the contrary he kept talking about the forthcoming exams and their importance for our future.

How could Mukund be so insensitive?

How can a young Indian deliberately keep his eyes and ears closed towards the chaos going on in the country, where thousands and lakhs of people had deviated from their path and were going haywire. They were unable to decide what to do next in life!

Was this the same Mukund, my friend, with whom I could discuss anything for hours together? When Mukund left abruptly without helping or comforting me with some assurance or support, I was dismayed and totally nonplussed. I couldn't sleep that night. I just kept on thinking about the next step to be taken now. When I woke up late the next morning, Banvari Bhaiya had already left.

However, I felt no bitterness against him. I continued to brood over and realised that Mukund's thought process and decision was the result of his upbringing. Perhaps I should consider my education too.

I decided to meet him once again and thinking that studying would provide me stablity to think rationally about my future.

After taking this decision, I was about to leave for the college and meet Mukund, when I noticed a book lying on the table. It was the Hindi translation of a Bengali book, which read 'Bandi Jeevan' (A Life of Captivity) by Shachindranath Sanyal. I picked it up and browsed through its pages.

Of course, Banvari Bhaiya must be reading it. Just then Banvari Bhaiya entered the house. 'Which is this book?' I was curious.

'Oh, this? It's very precious. I would say, a path-finder book for many like us.'

I requested Banvari Bhaiya to lend it to me when he completed reading it. Instead, he gave it to me immediately.

I was overjoyed. Perhaps answer to my dilemma was hidden in this book. Dropping the idea of meeting Mukund, I returned to my room and started reading the 'Bandi Jeevan.'

Just the way Banvari Bhaiya had mentioned, it was a book which spoke of sufferings of the freedom fighters and their crusade against the British Raj.

The book conveyed profound and motivating messages for those who wanted to do something to free their country from the Britishers.

All of a sudden, my confusion was gone! I forgot everything and was totally engrossed in reading the book.

I found myself strangely attracted to it and finished reading it by the next morning. It was like touching a volcano from inside. The words and thoughts of Shachindranath stirred something within me. I felt ignited and extremely motivated.

As I turned pages of the book, a gradual realisation dawned upon me about what I had been missing out all this time.

Banvari Bhaiya could see the effect of 'Bandi Jeevan' on me. He asked, 'So how did you find this book Bagga?'

I could not feign my excitement. 'It is an eye-opener Bhaiya. I have finished reading it already.'

Banvari Bhaiya smiled. (A smile of satisfaction). This was a rare sight on my brother's face.

'There are many such books in our college library, if you want to read more, you can contact Babulal, the second librarian there.'

I decided to visit the college library without wasting any time and meet Babulal the same day for more books.

Unlike every day, I did not stop by to pick up Mukund from his house for the college.

As I entered the college library, I saw a thin, inconspicuous looking person sitting at the front desk reading a book. I guessed that he was Babulal himself. Interestingly I had never noticed his presence in the library before.

Babulal was a short person, with a sad expression.

He got up and shook hands with me. Though there was nothing exceptional in his personality, I found him to be strangely familiar, someone I could rely upon.

I introduced myself, 'Satish.'

He smiled and replied, 'I know, You are Banvari's brother, right?'

I nodded. 'I have read 'Bandi Jeevan' and am really moved. I want you to give me some more good books.'

Babulal looked at me with interest. 'Which other books have you read?'

I was not an avid reader, other than studies, but talking about books always excited me.

'I have read only a few books by Swami Vivekananda. I also want to read Satyarth Prakash.I have heard a lot about this book. However, my ideals are Lenin and Stalin and I want to read their life stories as well.'

I felt Babulal was impressed with my answer. He smiled approvingly.

He took me to a remote corner of the library where stakes of real powerful reading stuff was kept, hidden from eyes of the students and the staff.

I was very ecstatic to see this. Here was a treasure lying inside our college and I never knew about it.

Babulal selected two books about the freedom struggle of Ireland and Russia. I took them for reading with his permission. I was exhilerated.

I thanked him profusely. He promised to give me more of such books for reading whenever I wanted.

I reached home in a happy mood. Banvari Bhaiya must have guessed that I had met Babulal but did not say anything. I went back to the library again after two days and got hold of some more motivational books by the great leaders of the world.

The books that I had started reading infused a new energy into my thinking and provided immense clarity towards my purpose in life.

I had a realisation that I should waste no more time now.

Strangely, Banvari Bhaiya had always given an impression of being a quiet and an indifferent person, although it was a mask under which was hidden a very determined person who was connected with the right people.

Suddenly I thought of Mukund, whom I was avoiding deliberately since a few days, and strange enough, had no regrets about it.

It was after a week when Banvari Bhaiya had asked me to accompany him to the college. This was very unusual.

I asked him, 'Is there anything important Bhaiya? Why do you want me to come with you?'

Banvari Bhaiya calmly replied, 'Nothing special Bagga. Just that Babulal has called us in the Library today morning.'

I was very curious to find out what was going to happen in the library. Banvari Bhaiya too did not seem to be knowing about it either.

As we entered the library, we were signalled to go to the backside by Babulal.

Banvari Bhaiya and I were not alone there. There were many other students and non-students waiting there, perhaps the ones who were selected for some mission.

However, the mission was not announced to us so far.

One professor started speaking in a soft voice, explaining to us importance of the occasion. This was exciting.

Till now, I did not know if there were any like-minded people, who could take the needed action. But looking at all this, it was not difficult to understand magnitude of the movement that was taking place in the college itself!

As the speaker continued to speak there was a feeling of alarm in the atmosphere. Something serious was going to take place.

Then he casually mentioned that certain leaflets had arrived from the Provincial Congress Committee Headquarters.

In the end, he asked us if we would help him in distributing the leaflets. He immediately added the warning that this might lead to our arrest, if we had a confrontation with the police.

It was understood that these pamphlets should reach the people of Hindustan, if possible and to the officers of the King too, but without any of us being caught by the police.

Babulal was ready with the pamphlets which had to be distributed.

Both Banvari Bhaiya and me gave our consent for distributing them.

The professor quietly went back to the college building after the talk was over.

The group present there swarmed around Babulal, who was assigning the different areas to everyone.

"Banvari, you go to the railway station, and Satish, you can go to the Residency," Babulal said.

These parts of the city were not easy to approach and it wouldn't be easy to avoid being noticed, as they were under constant surveillance by the British Police.

The pamphlets were now being distributed among the group members. I was thrilled.

It was like touching a live wire, or something as pious as God's writing.

This would mark the beginning of my life as a revolutionary.

I was convinced that this is how a fight should begin for the country's freedom.

For the first time, I felt proud of myself, knowing that they had good faith in us, only I did not know who 'they' were.

Banvari Bhaiya seemed excited too, but he could conceal his feelings. He looked calm as ever.

I soon understood that he was worried about me, as it was a completely new experience for me which involved risk. Moreover, I lacked the awareness necessary for such a mission.

He kept on asking me if I would be able to manage this distribution safely.

I laughed his concern off and promised to take care of myself. I whispered, "Do not worry Bhaiya! I know all the lanes and bylanes, if I need to run away."

But Banvari Bhaiya insisted upon changing the locations, and decided that I should go to the Railway station instead and he would take care of the Residency.

This was a small change or modification, and I did not mind it, as far as I was part of the whole scenario. I immediately consented to his proposal.

This minor change saved me from coming into the eyes of the British Police. On the other hand, Banvari Bhaiya had to pay a heavy price for it. There was another significant point amiss in our preparing for this mission.

We did not read the pamphlets properly and fully. The irony of the situation did not dawn upon us then.

All along we were unaware of what was written in the pamphlets. Perhaps that was what the professor was instructing about earlier in the library.

But it was too late by the time either of us thought and did something about it.

It contained a warning to the Government in harsh and blunt language, saying that insensitivity in treating the farmers and the citizens of India would not be tolerated anymore. There were a few other warnings too.

These writings were prepared with the idea of creating unrest among the masses, especially after the Non-Cooperation Movement was called off.

> *It was certainly a hasty and impulsive step on the part of those who were following up on these National issues, considering the fact that hardly a week had gone by after the suspension of the movement.*

I felt as if I was carrying a magic torch.

I was so overwhelmed that I almost started running towards the railway station.

Let me admit that in a gusto of excitement, I forgot to behave calmly. I made a mess of the wonderful opportunity that had fallen into my lap.

This is how it all happened. I had covered the leaflets in a newspaper.

When I reached my destination in about half an hour, I started to run here and there in excitement, without any clarity about how to carry out this imposing task.

Banvari Bhaiya was right about me. Having no experience in such a mission which asks for presence of mind, alertness and appropriate execution, I couldn't do justice to the given opportunity.

I had a big bunch of leaflets with me to be distributed.

At first, I thought it was a good idea to stick some flyers on the walls, but didn't know how risky this could be. Moreover, how was I to stick them?

I wasn't carrying any adhesive for this purpose, so I had to abandon the idea.

I ran from passenger to passenger who were travelling, and started handing over the pamphlets to them.

Not that everyone accepted it, many threw them right away. For others it had no importance, and people either walked past or ignored me.

Overall, the leaflets did not seem to be creating any effect. Perhaps illiteracy came into their way.

After some time, a few people started reading them with curiosity, and realised that this was a serious matter. They started looking at me with somewhat shocked and surprised expressions.

Some persons threw the pamphlets away immediately, whereas the others hurriedly got away from the place.

> *It was not entirely my fault when in a hurry to reach the flyers to as many people as possible, a major bulk dropped down from my hands and fell on the railway tracks, scattered all over.*

Incidentally, this was the old Lucknow Railway Station, the platform was small and its height was uneven at various places.

(New and grand Lucknow railway station was built almost two years later.)

I was dismayed and hated myself for being clumsy.

As an obvious gesture to save the dropped leaflets, I decided to get down on the tracks and collect as many as I could.

Just as I was about to jump down, two men pulled me back, and signalled that a train was fast approaching the station on the same tracks. In fact, it was already entering the platform.

I had to stop. I was very disheartened, and cursing myself at the same time.

How I wished to be more careful and patient in accomplishing the task! But it was too late now.

As the train halted at the station, several passengers got down, with the coolies running to reach them to help their luggage being unloaded from the train.

Alas! This was taking longer than I had imagined.

As luck would have it, Lucknow was the final destination for this train, so it would take longer to send it to the yards, for cleaning, and preparing for its next journey.

It was no use waiting for the train
to be moved from there now and
pick up the flyers then.

Besides, it was very certain that these flyers might be spoilt and were useless now.

I stood there helplessly for a few moments, witnessing a golden opportunity turning into a waste just because of my carelessness.

The Railway Station was far from my house, so I took lanes and bylanes to reach home quickly. It took me almost an hour.

A bigger shock was waiting for me there.

Birendra, the ever-ready messenger, came running to me. He almost shouted amid his heavy breaths, "Uncle Bagga (he stopped for breath)...Uncle...Banvari is arrested."

This was shocking. What went wrong with Banvari Bhaiya?

I asked Birendra, "Biru, how did you come to know? Who told you? Which police station is he taken to?"

"Uncle, as I was returning from the grocery store, I happened to pass by Lalaji's shop. He called me to inform about all this. Uncle Banvari has been taken to the Residency Police Station."

Nothing had looked so risky when we had parted for distributing the leaflets, which could put Banvari Bhaiya behind the bars. What happened then?

Without questioning further, I went to the kitchen, washed my hands and after drinking a glass of water rushed out of the house.

Biru wanted to come along but I prevented him saying, "Biru, you should stay at home. Just in case Mataji or Leela might need you."

I decided to meet Lalaji on way. Since he already knew about Banvari Bhaiya, he could be of some help or aleast could advise something in this regard.

I reached Lalaji's shop in less than ten minutes, almost running on the way.

"Lalaji, what has happened? Where is Banvari Bhaiya?"

Lalaji looked disturbed too. "Bete, (Son) Banvari and few others let it loose. Rajaji ke aadmion ne ghera daal diya." (King's men cornered them)

What a folly! But I was certain that Banvari Bhaiya could tackle such risky situations.

"Mai usse se mil kar aata hoon." (I will go and meet him) Lalaji looked disturbed and apprehensive.

"Sambhalke. Kahin tum unke haath na pad jana." (Take care. You don't get trapped.) Lalaji finished making a paan, (Betel leaf) and handed over to me.

This was for keeping my spirits high. I could not deny.

After some time as I was hurrying towards the police station, I saw Pitaji rushing towards me from the other side of the road.

Alas! This was the last thing I could have imagined to happen. And there was no possibility or use of hiding myself from him. In fact, this was not the time for him to return from the office, I realised. He was early by an hour.

I was speechless. Pitaji came closer, and held my hand. In a weak voice he said, "Let us go to the police station where Banvari is taken to."

How did he come to know about this incident? It was futile to say anything now.

I was deeply touched by his sad and worried tone. I realised how concerned are the parents about their children and how strong their support can be. I gladly agreed. His presence would help both Banvari and myself.

My mind was stormy. I was anxious and impatient to reach the police station as soon as possible, but with father accompanying, I had to move at his pace with no other choice.

All this while, I was thinking over various solutions to help Banvari Bhaiya get released from the police station without any indictment.

He had definitely not committed any crime, but was only involved in distribution of the pamphlets. I was certain that he would be released soon after a strict warning or a minor punishment by the Magistrate.

Pitaji and I reached the Residency Police Station in some time.

अब न पिछले वलवले हैं और न अरमानों की भीड़।

❑

Aftermath of the Adventure

Banvari Narrates

Luckily Satish escaped from going to the jail. Nobody from our family had been jailed till today. It was me who got imprisoned for the first time.

For a simple offence like distributing the pamphlets against the British Government.

I had not expected this to happen to me. In fact, I was all the while worried about Satish.

After we separated to distribute the pamphlets, I took the road to the Residency as decided with Bagga.

When I reached the area of action near the Residency, there was not much of a crowd.

A few vendors were selling miscellaneous things. Few women, some with children, were shopping. All were Indians, and appeared to be the locals.

Around the Residency, one could come across the British people roaming about with their families, since this part of Lucknow had a history and the strong memories of the 1857 mutiny.

The siege of Lucknow was a prolonged defence for the Residency within the city of Lucknow during the Indian Rebellion of 1857.

Only after two successive relief attempts had reached the city, the defenders and the civilians could be evacuated from the Residency, which was later abandoned.

It was more than 50 years before that the war between the British and the Indians had taken place here.

Life had slowly started seeping back in this otherwise peaceful but dull place with a sprawling garden, and was frequented by people in the evenings.

However, this was not the time of the day when one could find people, let alone the Gora log. The air was still warm, and it was not yet evening.

I started distributing the pamphlets to people on the road, and in the shops nearby. Most of them started throwing them away carelessly and reacting as if they were mere advertisement leaflets.

I felt disappointed. How could I explain the importance of these leaflets to them?

Having gathered some courage, I decided to go inside the Residency nonchalantly.

The place was a long stretch of a green garden, with two or three buildings, which narrated the saga of the war fought. There were various marks of the bullets and the dilapidation in the walls. I continued to distribute the leaflets to a few people who were sitting there on the benches and they seemed to take interest. Some of them started reading the leaflets seriously.

After some time, their curiosity seemed to be increasing due to the content. Soon a small crowd gathered around me. Interestingly, some of them also demanded for additional pamphlets from me. It was a moment of complascence for me.

In all probability, police were likely to be there in the vicinity. Obviously, they would be extra cautious to avoid any disturbance in the Residency area.

As expected, not much time had elapsed when the police arrived on the scene, as they saw a crowd gathered there.

It was so foolish of Babulal not to have warned me to run away from the scene as soon as my work was done. Besides, it was my own stupidity that I kept hanging around to enjoy the stir created among the people and feel like a hero. The police did not disturb the crowd from reading the pamphlets, but asked them who had distributed them.

Suddenly a policeman in civilian clothes advanced towards me and asked me to accompany him.

For me it was an ultimate success to be noticed by the police. Though I was always mentally prepared for this sinister encounter, it took me a few seconds to grasp the reality.

I cheerfully accompanied the policeman, worrying about Satish at the same time.

What must have happened to him? Could he distribute the pamphlets properly and safely?

I kept on praying that all went well with Bagga.

We reached the Residency Police Station, which was one of the important police stations of Lucknow. I saw many students being caught by the police in the same manner and being brought there. I looked around anxiously for Bagga.

> *A gush of relief spread over my mind to see that he was not among the other students who were captured with me. Many were shouting slogans "Mahatma Gandhi ki Jai" and ""Bharat Mata ki Jai".*

It was indeed disappointing to see Gandhi calling off the Non-Cooperation Movement, which had resulted in all this mess. Unfortunately, like the thousands of innocent and aspiring young boys, I too was victimised.

Nonetheless, I was in the police station now.

I felt a strange thrilling sensation. It was almost the feel of attaining the independence already.

Alas! My feeling of victory was fake, just an illusion, which I realised within a few minutes.

I was given a chair and allowed to sit in a corner. No one could see me from outside. The details such as my name, father's name, some identification marks, etc. were noted in a printed form. My signature and thumb prints were taken too.

I saw a group of other boys entering the police station who had participated in the distribution of the pamphlets or had carried out some other anti-government acts for which they were brought there.

A similar procedure of filling up of the forms was carried out with them.

In a moment of realisation, I felt that I was actually facing the British Government, and had won half the battle against them already.

It indeed was a good beginning for me, a certainty that I was ready to challenge them in future.

All the boys arrested were grouped together. Many hours had passed since we were taken into custody.

I didn't know any of the boys personally, but soon the feeling of camaraderie prevailed among us. After talking to them, I came to know about the true objective behind the distribution of the pamphlets.

It was a mission intelligently planned by the leaders of the revolutionary groups who were helped by some Congress leaders. Its objective was to serve a notice to the British Government.

It was not restricted to Lucknow alone, but had spread over three other cities – Agra, Delhi and Allahabad also.

The procedure to imprison us was now in process besides the other formalities. Some preliminaries of the law were being carried out.

We were to be transferred to the district prison so we were taken out. Our destiny now lay in the hands of the mighty British Government. Anxiety and preparing myself for accepting this challenge were the two things weighing upon my mind at that moment.

As I stepped out of the police station, to my great relief, I saw Satish standing with our father, patiently waiting for me.

A big crowd had gathered after the news of arrest of the revolutionaries spread like fire. My face brightened, but Bagga looked pained to see me as a prisoner.

On the other hand, a feeling of helplessness prevailed upon me, and I was almost in tears to see my old Pitaji waiting there with Satish.

There was a very little opportunity to talk, as we passed through the crowd to board the carriage. It would be wiser not to do so, lest they would be questioned and involved in the whole issue.

I continued to walk with the other captives.

After some time, Bagga managed to come closer to me and whispered whether I wanted to be released on bail. I refused, not knowing its implications, but that is what one was supposed to do, I guessed. Soon we were to board a carriage that would take us to the jail.

All these experiences were completely new to me. I was eager to find out what awaited us behind the walls of the jail.

I turned back to see Pitaji and Satish. I could see father turning and walking away with slow steps, Bagga hurriedly holding him, both on their way home.

This must be a huge shock for father. I did not know how much he knew about the things that Bagga and I had got into.

I wished I could read his thoughts about my adventure or should I say daredevil act, but it was too late now.

Thinking about Bagga, I got a feeling that he might be regretting not being with me at this crucial moment. I rather felt relieved.

Then for no reason, I remembered Satish's friend, Mukund.

Strange it was to see how indifferent he looked the last time when we met, considering the fact that he was Bagga's close friend. Irrespective of that, my gut feeling told me that our family might need his support in future.

Soon the carriage came to a halt in front of the Central Jail.

Probably the prison officers had already been informed about our arrival, and were waiting for us.

But as per their nature, they grumbled saying that it was very late.

As the barracks were locked before the sunset, we were hurried through the ceremonies. We were searched thoroughly for weapons as well as money, if at all we were carrying something.

After this was over, police left us in
the hands of the prison officers and
same formalities were followed for
the registration of our identities.

Before being sent to the barracks, each prisoner was supplied with a small iron plate, a bowl, one bedding and two rough blankets. This was going to be my property during the jail stay.

I learnt later, even these items were likely to be stolen in the closed boundaries of the prison walls. I could not figure out if this was a funny situation or a tragic one.

Next, we were led to a water tap and asked to scrub the utensils and collect the food that was ready for us. We did not feel like obeying the warder's orders.

Each experience was strange and new for me.

Perhaps the Warder wanted to finish off his work soon, so he asked an undertrial to do it.

We were served with the jail-bread and a foul-smelling vegetable. The bread was gritty. I had not eaten for hours, but the stench was so repelling that I couldn't eat.

Was it the smell of urine? No, it was just the badly cooked vegetables that gave out such a smell. Eventually, a sense of heroism prevailed upon me and in that state of mind, I finished the so called 'food' provided to us.

I was settling down mentally, once the gush of heroism and adventure subsided.

Before long I realised that this was completely a different world and different laws applied here. There was hierarchy, favouritism and prejudices involved at every stage.

A convict overseer was designated for each barrack. He would instruct us about the jail rules and if the things were not okay, he had the authority to complain or punish the inmates. One who was in charge of us appeared to be liberal and did not mind our talking to each other, in other words gossiping, although honestly speaking this was against the rules.

He would gently warn us that we should retire to our berths else our belongings would be stolen.

I found that talking to others may throw some light on what was happening all around, and had an opportunity to find out who were the other arrestees and I tried to connect with them.

Much to my delight, there were known faces from my college who were arrested and were with me in this prison.

I was also surprised to see some boys who appeared to be always busy with studies in the college and never cared about freedom issues then, were here too.

There were many senior intelligent freedom fighters who were jailed with us.

In fact, there were also undertrials, but they did not take much interest in us. They just looked at us from a distance. We somehow carried an image of the violent rebels, without any aggressive behaviour on our part.

There was no point in trying to start any conversation with them for the time being.

As the shadow of night started spreading, one of the greatest revealations about this prison reached me through some fellow prisoners.

Strangely, there was one friend of the prisoners in the jail itself, who could help us get almost anything and everything in the jail!

This was unbelievable.

People outside the jail campus would consider this to be a myth and refrain from believing. But this was true, and obviously a blessing in the surroundings of a lost world. It did not take long for the supplier to learn about us, the new entrants to the jail that the message had reached us. It was not easy to succumb immediately to his offers without knowing how genuine he was. But other inmates assured us of his credibility.

> *He had a list of things that could be provided inside the four walls without creating any offence at the police level or risking the prisoner's safety.*

There was also a provision for sending messages to our relatives. This brought a smile of relief on the faces of all the new prisoners. The things were not that bad after all.

We hesitatingly inquired if we could establish connection with the other political prisoners there. The reply was in positive and within no time we got almost all the information about them.

We were also told that soon we might join them in the jail after our trials. This indeed was very encouraging.

Once we could establish contacts with the political prisoners, a lot of information could be obtained from them, that in which direction the freedom struggle was proceeding.

To be honest, I was very excited to be labelled as a freedom fighter in the jail at this moment. I found it impossible to sleep in these circumstances at night. I suggested that all of us should sit together and talk throughout the night, but that was strictly prohibited. This is where we had to draw the line.

Not only that, after a while we were advised to disperse by an overseer convict.

The night went by in darkness and thinking about Bagga, Leela, parents, and Babulal. Their faces ran through my mind and the whole drama of I being captured and brought to the jail kept appearing in front of my eyes, and I did not realise when I went off to sleep.

As the new day began, I learnt that the jails also had a very fixed routine, which started by getting up early in the morning. We were more of the onlookers and not toiling like the other prisoners, which albeit would be our fate very soon, as the trial would begin.

Since we were undertrial prisoners, presently, stricter rules did not apply to us.

Neverthless, it was equally important to stay in the jail for a few days to know in depth how the British Government operated things.

With all the time in the world at my disposal, I started observing the equation between the political and the non-political prisoners, which was not a normal one. Funny enough, non- political prisoners looked at their counterparts as if the ones who had come were their saviours.

It was an undisputed fact that our fight was against injustice and inhumanity, which was a habitual system adopted by the British Government against all Indian civilians and they wanted these cruel systems to prevail in the jail as well.

In short, every move that we made or reaction we showed towards the system of the jail, caught the attention and interest of the non- political prisoners, and somewhere in their mind they were certain that our protests or dislikes would be beneficial for them directly or indirectly.

All of us i.e., the students and the other boys who were imprisoned for the pamphlet distribution, were kept in the jail for almost four days before the trial began.

D-day dawned and we were asked to prepare ourselves for the trial. In a little while, we were to be produced in front of the magistrate.

As we were taken from the prison to the local court of Lucknow, we could see that a large crowd had gathered to see the trial.

I looked for the familiar faces, and suddenly I could see my father, Bagga and Babulal anxiously waiting in the crowd which had gathered there. In fact, there were many relatives who had come to see their kin released. No one appeared to be in panic, as it was a routine trial.

A local school with its teachers and students was there to cheer us up as if it was a football match in which we were taking part. Nonetheless, this thrilled us.

A cordon of policemen was formed around us. Thus, we entered the court room.

Our case was to be tried by the Prosecution Lawyer, Mr. Khare.

He entered the Court room from the other direction. He was unmoved by the slogans and the crowd and remained expressionless throughout the whole procedure. He knew his job well.

The court proceedings started.

> *A message was sent to us by someone in the courtroom, that we should boycott the court proceedings by not recognising it. If we did not cooperate with the court from the beginning, they would not be able to charge us of any lawlessness.*

Though we all found it to be a heroic approach, it was a blunder on our part. The Court was prepared in advance to decide against us. They had already prepared a trap to frame us.

Before we could understand or grasp the situation, much to our shock, we were charged with obstructing the traffic.

The legal brains of British Government had very skillfully cooked up this whole set-up, and that created a completely different scenario in front of the court and the people present there.

We all realised that the situation was slipping out of our hands.

My biggest mistake was that, not even once did I try to know what was the matter printed in the pamphlets. It was too late now.

I came to know from one arrestee that one of the signatories on these pamphlets was a famous leader. If it was disclosed to the court about the pamphlets, then they would in addition have to arrest the person who had written this.

It was an irony that the Government played the dirty games of favouritism.

Since we were instructed not to recognise the court, we had not appointed any lawyer to defend us as well. We were completely mistaken in realising the power of the court. It was so easy for them to trap us with mere lies and fake charges.

There was no question of defence, even if we had excitedly planned for any. The court had obviously presented well prepared witnesses. Their statements were taken accordingly, who confidently stated that we were obstructing the traffic. Everything was staged perfectly.

No further questions were asked in this one-sided trial.

That was the end of it, since there was no lawyer to cross-examine the witnesses about the details of the event.

I tried to read the audience's mind watching the proceedings, and could see that this had greatly disturbed Satish and a few others, who were allowed to sit in the courtroom.

When these fake charges and the sham proceedings were going on, Satish got up from his place and started shouting, 'This is a farce! This is a lie!'

Listening to him, few others too got up and joined him.

I was frightened to see Satish's reaction, lest he would be arrested too. Luckily their shouts died away before long. Satish and all others were safe.

Ironically, the Magistrate feigned to be fair and just. He called us one by one to make a statement to show that he gave us equal opportunity to speak in our favour, as the trial was thoroughly genuine.

As decided, each of us said that this was the same Government who was responsible for the Jallianwala massacre and we would not recognise the British Court or the Government. Hence, we had nothing to say.

Unfortunately, this turned out to be helpful in the court proceedings. Consequently, the trial was shortened due to our non-cooperation. All the arrestees gave such vague statements that the court was adjourned for a few minutes.

Then it was the judgement time.

Soon Mr. Khare re-appeared and announced three months' simple imprisonment for each one of us. Some of the senior arrestees were sentenced for six months imprisonment for the same offence.

The people found this to be a heroic gesture. The news of our conviction was welcomed by the crowd which was patiently waiting outside the court. We became heroes all of a sudden.

People cheered for us. It felt so strange to see, how mass psyche worked. Looking at the reaction of the people, the police was alarmed, and hurriedly wanted to pack us off to the jail, where we were to stay for at least 3 months.

I was dazed by what had happened in the courtroom. A series of stupid decisions and carelessness had resulted in the convenient trial for the British Court as they wanted it to be.

Neverthless, my patriotic feeling prevailed over a thoughtful behaviour, and I resigned to the decision of the court and fell an easy prey to their sly plans. Among the hustle-bustle of bringing us out from the court, Satish somehow managed to squeeze through the crowd, and came near me to ask about the bail, but I refused.

In fact, section 107 under which we were convicted allowed us to be bailed out, if we wanted. I could offer sureties, but this would have violated my position as a non-cooperator. Besides, I myself did not want to be bailed out.

I had made a promise to myself during the Non-Cooperation Movement not to appear weak in front of the Government, and would continue to keep the promise even today.

All those who were convicted, were cheered up and labelled as heroes by the people, and were escorted upto the prison gates.

It was amusing to see that there were many volunteers, eager to join us by getting arrested.

The situation was certainly not normal, and this irritated the police there.

This was that glorious period of the Indian politics, when a crowd accompanying an arrested leader and escorting him up to the prison gates insisted on being imprisoned en masse.

The police tried to control the crowd sternly. They ordered the people to stay away. But they could not stop them from shouting,

'Bharat Mata ki Jai!' ('Hail Mother India!')

(This was the time when there were no other slogans to show resentment against the Government. The slogan of 'Jai Hind' was made popular later by Babu Subhash Chandra Bose, and that of 'Inquilab Zindabad' by Bhagat Singh, who joined us in a few years.)

As we returned to the same prison, now as residents there, our barracks were changed.

They were not very far from where we were put initially.

It appeared that this was the time when the prisons were filled with the new political prisoners everyday, and it was natural that their strength was in the majority in comparison to the non-political prisoners.

The atmosphere inside the prison was more like a huge assembly. As soon as the new political prisoners entered, they were greeted with the slogans like 'Bharat Mata ki Jay!' ('Hail Mother India!') and 'Mahatma Gandhi ki Jay! '('Hail Mahatma Gandhi!') which echoed from every corner.

This continued for almost an hour for each prisoner, till he settled down, irrespective of the community he belonged to. Certainly, this was a very warm welcome.

In fact, being in the prison updated us with a lot of news about the national scenario regarding the freedom movement, and different leaders.

Since Gandhi was in the jail, and the Non-Cooperation Movement was snubbed, the possibility of a violent fight back, which had worried the British Government, had subsided now.

This was when, we heard about a
boy named Chandrashekhar.

When he was asked about his name during a trial for some offence against the Government, he had replied, 'Azad '(free), father's name 'Swadhin' (independent) and the residence 'Prison'. This was enough to invite wrath of the court.

Such fearless and unexpected replies enraged the magistrate and instead of sending him to the jail, he ordered him to be whipped severely. Even the strongest of the criminals shuddered at this punishment, but here was Chandrashekhar, who after each whip shouted 'Mahatma Gandhi ki Jay!'('Hail Mahatma Gandhi!')

This incident made him famous as 'Chandrashekhar Azad'. He earned spontaneous popularity among the people.

The Freedom Movement outside had gathered momentum, as a consequence of which, we occupied a bigger portion of the prison.

Within a couple of weeks, the political prisoners began to flood the prison.

There were many issues in the prison, where an apparent partiality was shown towards some prisoners, whereas the political prisoners were rendered unfair treatment and in many jails, confronted with the vengeance too.

There were many rules we did not agree to. The first was that being ordinary prisoners, we were not supposed to talk to anybody. This and many other rules had been rejected by us on the very first day.

Every barrack or every two barracks had a sort of compound surrounded by 8- or 9-feet high walls. We had full freedom of movement inside the compound.

However, barred gates of the compound were kept locked and no political prisoner was allowed in and out until officially required at the jail gate for interviews etc.

However, jumping over the walls stealthily, to talk to the prisoners on the other side, and returning in the same manner was constantly done by the political prisoners. It had assumed the shape of a movement.

Even the ordinary prisoners were on the verge of mutiny. Everyday a good number of political prisoners coming in had literally made the system apprehensive.

The officials were afraid to see the ever-growing number of the prisoners inside the jail, in addition to what was going on outside. The Freedom Movement might succeed after all.

Ultimately, they made a compromise. They conceded that at specified hours, we would be allowed to interact and move about as we pleased. It was soon felt that regulating the hours was not possible, so that the gates were eventually kept open during the day time. Thus, this battle was won.

Another such harassing issue was the gritty bread being served to us. Next, we diverted our attention to this problem. The majority of the political prisoners were quite indifferent towards this aspect, considering it to be a part of the intentional game played by the British Government to humiliate them.

However, there were many who could not tolerate it, happening this twice a day.

> *Nothing was pre-arranged to fight against this, but one fine day, when the bread was distributed, one political prisoner hurled his share into the air, followed by his metal plates, which were his only utensils.*

Immediately hundreds of chapattis along with the plates were flying into the air. Even our leaders in the jail were dragged into this movement soon. This turned out to be a great advantage for us.

Since our leaders were involved in today's incidence, to our great surprise, the ceasefire followed faster than expected. Our leaders said a representation should be sent and the officials should be given a chance to improve. Though this was only for the time being, eventually the movement subsided in our prison. Unfortunately, this problem was applicable to all the prisons under the British rule. In future, it was destined to become a major fight carried out by many freedom fighters. The dedicated martyrs like Jatindranath Das sacrificed their lives, and others like Bhagat Singh, Mahavir Singh and hundreds of other boys had to go through horrifying experiences while fasting for their principles.

All these efforts were not going to solve our problems in the long run.

For example, the quality of the bread had improved, and the pulse was a little thicker. Some political prisoners were also given little milk on the medical grounds, that was all.

Conversely, our elders felt that we should make a constructive use of the time on hand and not waste energies and fighting spirit merely for our small rights, gossips or loitering around all the time in the jail.

The authorities decided to start various classes in the jail, which they felt, would keep the prisoners occupied and provide a positive thoughtfulness.

There were many learned scholars like Sampurnanand, J.B.Kripalani and a few others, who could give good lectures and divert our minds from the fighting mode against the British system.

Sampuranand was proficient in teaching various aspects of the Bhagwad Gita. Soon his classes were a great success and the most prisoners looked forward to attending them irrespective of their religion. Many of us felt it was like visiting a temple. All of us were attracted towards spirituality in one way or the other after listening to his lectures.

Prof. Kripalani was the lecturer in the other class. He lectured us on the book 'Duties of Man' by Mazzini. He would read a para from this book, and then elaborate the topic for almost an hour. Unlike the spiritual lectures by Sampurnanand where sacrificing was glorified, Kripalani focussed, and criticised the caste-ridden Hindu ways of life. His views were very radical, and gave a good food for thought to all of us, of course a bit differently.

In the early 1920s, these were certainly very revolutionary thoughts from every point of view, and his lectures also created a lot of awareness regarding the social issues of the Indian society. However, not many agreed with his thinking, and his lectures were attended sparsely.

Apart from these two luminaries, there were some budding writers and intellectuals such as Kamalapati, Vichitranarain, Raghunath Singh, Jogendra Shukla and some others.

They all decided to start a handwritten Hindi weekly named 'Karagar' under the editorship of Ugra, who was a well-known writer himself. Thankfully, this was allowed in the prison.

I was called upon to write in Hindi.

Our journal and the classes brought about a pleasant change in almost every political prisoner's approach and changed the direction of our activities.

From the destructive, we went over to the creative realm. We took to more and more reading and writing.

I started learning Marathi from Baba Raghavdas, which proved helpful.

In turn, I started teaching Hindi to some Bengali prisoners. This was very easy for me, and many prisoners did it very happily.

With a calm mind now, we shifted our focus to the actual situation in the prison. There were many genuine issues which needed to be taken care of.

Many political prisoners were sentenced to a rigorous imprisonment, where they had to twist the moonj (from the coconut peel) fibre into 300 yards of thin rope, and this task had to be completed by the evening.

In fact, this was also a popular punishment inflicted upon the prisoners at the Cellular jail in Andaman- Nicobar Islands, and no excuse helped in escaping from it. We were the fortunate ones who weren't subjected to such a punishment. Once when this task of twisting the moonj was assigned to the selected political prisoners, they did not take notice of it, and it was left undone.

Then someone gave a brilliant idea, 'Why don't we make a bon- fire of it?'

And this was implemented immediately.

Next day no fibre was sent. Eventually, this punishment was ruled out by the authorities. Thus, the punishment of labour came to an end in our jail in a single stroke.

There was one more problem that a convict had to wear something like an iron necklace round his neck with a rectangular piece of wood attached to it. The registration number of the convict, the section under which he was convicted, his period of punishment and the date of release were embossed on it.

Every convict was supposed to wear this. They called it the neck ticket. It was the most humiliating thing as it looked exactly like a dog collar with a licence number.

It was natural that the political prisoners would not wear this. The non-political prisoners also followed our footsteps so that this system was totally abolished after some time.

This was one of the permanent changes brought about during our imprisonment.

All these victories again, were negative in nature. We were told to do something, and we did not comply. This did not solve all our problems though.

We were jubilant to an extent but we had to bring about certain positive changes.

For example, the food that was provided to the prisoners became better in quality, but the diet did not improve, as the local authorities had no such power.

Finally, the political prisoners decided to carry out a hunger strike, which was brought to notice of the authorities, and the negotiations were carried out in alliance with the supporters for freedom outside.

After a few days, the Government enforced some classification on the prisoners.

The ultimate result of the hunger strikes in the prison and the agitation outside was that the Government created two classes of prisoners:

1. First class of the misdemeanants
2. Second class of the misdemeanants.

Incidentally, this was very helpful, as there was no standardisation of the same laws. The treatment of all the political prisoners entirely depended upon the magistrate's recommendation.

As my fate would have it, I was classified as the second-class prisoner. There was no option, but to accept what the order was.

When the jails had their own stories to tell, we were also updated about the happenings outside and on the national front.

> *The 'Civil Disobedience' (no-tax) campaign had already started in many districts of Madras, but many big leaders intervened and the issue was sorted out through the tax payments.*

There were many other issues taken up by our leaders as a part of the Civil Disobedience. The British Government continued stuffing the prisons with hundreds of the non-cooperative ones.

One famous Indian lawyer, who was representing the Government came up with a genius idea of salvaging the non-political laws and applying them against the non-cooperators.

This was a trick well played against the convicts, and resulted in a helpless situation to get them released on the factual grounds.

During all these activities and events, I did not realise that I was past my defined imprisonment a long time ago. I was almost past six months in the prison, and there was no sign of release, or for that matter, for all those who were jailed with me.

Finally, I decided to take up this matter with the jailor, who was a strict officer, but with fair values. He assured me that my case would be taken up and if it was found that there was no reason to detain me any further, I would be released soon.

Perhaps things were changing after all.

I started waiting for the golden moment when I would be free again and with my family members.

Satish Narrates

What the British Government did with Banvari Bhaiya and other arrestees was unbelievable.

I witnessed the proceedings at the local court, as the hearing was going on for Banvari Bhaiya's case. The accused were charged with the crime of obstructing the traffic, which was a blatant lie.

The legal brains of the British Government built an imaginary story –a sheer lie to trap the arrestees. The whole case was but a drama fabricated by them. This created a very wrong picture of the whole case and arrestees didn't have any opportunity to defend themselves.

Babulal, sitting next to me, showed a pamphlet, which I read from the beginning to the end. He pointed out something in the pamphlet, which had gone completely unnoticed by me and Banvari Bhaiya.

My eyes fell on the names given at the bottom of the memo.

How could we have missed this? Suddenly I realised the reason for all this drama, and looked at Babulal. He nodded in affirmation.

The Government was playing clever from its side. It was easier to jail an unknown crowd by enforcing wrong allegations on them, rather than imprisoning the known leaders and get into a controversy.

But, due to falsely crafted allegations, the situation got out of control. I tried to shout and draw the attention of the court during its proceedings, but that did not have any effect on the King's men. They had pre-decided the charges and slyly planned the desired outcome too.

I was so dazed to see all this, that I did not realise how speedily the remaining procedures were summed up, using set of lies, and fake witnesses against the group of so-called convicts, with Banvari Bhaiya being one of them.

There was no hope now to save my brother, as the case was already over.

I ran towards the group who were being taken to the jail, somehow, I reached near Banvari Bhaiya, threading my way through the cordon formed by the British Police.

Taking precaution not to be noticed, I whispered into his ear, “Do you want bail?”

The way he looked at me, I could clearly comprehend that asking him about the release was a futile effort.

I had already received my answer before he could even reply, which was obviously in negative.

In an instant I saw him vanishing from my sight, along with the other prisoners from the courtroom. I was feeling utterly helpless at that moment. For the first time, I experienced the brunt of power and position when they are in wrong hands, where there is no difference between truth and lie.

I returned to where Pitaji was sitting in the courtroom on the other side.

All this while I had forgotten about him.

I wondered what must be going through his mind while watching the drama of lies.

Surprisingly he looked composed or pretented to be. As I watched him, I noticed something unbelievable.

Did his eyes have a spark? A spark of pride, coming alive that seemed to have died a long time ago? I looked at him again.

Was this his own dream at some point of time in his life? This was a greater surprise to me. I had never known or given a thought to Pitaji's views on the freedom movement.

The secret was gradually unveiling now, what he felt was the reflection of his passion for India's freedom.

I was filled with pride for Pitaji unknowingly. I caught his hand, and helped him get up.

We returned home, with a heavy heart, without exchanging a word on the way back. Neither father nor I was in a mood to discuss anything presently. Mother and Leela were anxiously waiting for us.

Naturally, they were expecting to see Banvari Bhaiya, to be released and freed after the trial.

'Bagga Bhaiya, where is Banvari Bhaiya?' Leela asked. I could hardly face her.

Perhaps, she understood. She brought water for both of us from the kitchen.

On the other hand, mother always believed in the fate and accepted everything that happened in life without questioning. But today she also sounded agitated.

"Bagga, why my son is not released?" Her voice was trembling. I had no answer.

Pitaji was a man of few words. He just said, "Banvari was charged with a fake offence. He will be imprisoned for 3 months. He did not want to be bailed out."

Mother started crying as she learnt about Banvari Bhaiya, and rushed to the kitchen.

Leela quietly heard everything, and further asked some questions about the trial.

She seemed dazed. In fact, it was not easy for me to accept the reality as well.

Banvari Bhaiya was sentenced for 3 months' imprisonment. This was a warning signal for me.

It would not be easy, if I wanted to participate in the freedom struggle.

But then there was no possibility of giving it up either at this juncture.

I had met Babulal during the court proceedings, and he told me to take things lightly for a few days.

"The Police has its agents scattered all over the place", he said.

He further added, "Even the college library was being sealed. The news about the meeting and the leaflets being distributed by the students and others had come into the knowledge of the British Police. It would be wiser to keep away from the place and stay safe for some time."

About ten days later, I received a message from Babulal, to come and meet him in the college. He had sent the message via Lalaji Paanwala, who had a small shop in the heart of the market, on the road to the Chowk. One could not escape from being seen by him if he happened to pass from that street.

Lalaji used to sell paan and other miscellaneous items like candies, tobacco, etc. at his shop.

I often visited Lalaji's shop with Banvari Bhaiya to savour the paan (betel leaf). I recollected that he used to talk to both of us very fondly, especially Banvari Bhaiya.

In fact, he had conveyed the message of Banvari Bhaiya's arrest.

The boy who worked in his shop to assist him came to my house early in the morning after a week of

Banvari Bhaiya's court trial. He handed over a piece of paper to me.

Fortunately, nobody was around. I took the paper and wentquietly out in the backyard. It carried a simple message saying, "Your paan is ready."

I was puzzled.

Neither did I order any paan to Lalaji nor Banvari Bhaiya had told me anything about this.

But this message made me really excited and I looked forward to meet Lalaji as soon as possible. I was into the actual game now.

Around 11 a.m. I walked past his shop, and said casually, "Namaste!" (Hello!) to the old fellow.

He nodded and gave a smile which was more like confirming something. I waited to decode it. I then saw Babulal coming towards me.

Babulal and Lalaji? How were they connected?

It was indeed comforting to see that the two supporters from unexpected corners for a good cause were together.

Babulal told me to follow him. We reached the college campus in some time.

Babulal took me to the back of the college building.

We instantly came out of the college campus and continued to walk.

After some time, we reached a small hut like structure. "This is their Ashram, Satish," Babulal announced.

"Their?" I did not understand anything, but was very curious by now to see who they were.

We went closer and saw a few people, sitting on an old cot outside the hut.

They appeared like volunteers of the place.

One person waved Babulal to go. Two of them stayed back, and others who were sitting with them also got up and walked away.

I was left with the remaining two, who apparently were the leaders.

One person was tall and well built with a wheatish complexion, and appeared to be in mid-twenties. He seemed to be in complete command, which appeared from his way of speaking and body language.

The other person was almost the same age, little frail, fair and with sharp, observant eyes. Perhaps he was the advisor to the leader.

They seemed to be having all the information about me.

I had started writing a few articles in our college magazine lately, and they knew about it too.

The well built one was talking. “So your brother Banvari is in jail Satish?”

I nodded. They were updated with all the news.

He continued, “We would like to know how interested you are in joining our group?”

I did not know what to answer. Perhaps I was not sure.

The other person added hastily. “Panditji, please give him time to decide. We can not push anyone by force.”

Panditji seemed to agree, "Yes, Guruji!" Then turning towards me, he added,

"Bagga, I am happy that you helped us in distributing the pamphlets. But the challenge ahead is not an easy one for us."

So they knew my nick-name as well.

Then they bombarded me with questions on my political thoughts.

This was unexpected. I knew some answers, and many I did not know, about which I accepted frankly.

After half an hour of interrogation, I was allowed to leave. This was an experience of a lifetime for me.

To believe in something is one thing, but to take an action on it is completely different.

I reached home with the same mental turmoil. I was unable to sleep and kept on thinking about today's experience all night.

Who were these two persons? Both looked fully aware with whatever was happening nationally, and were in control of their activities and plans.

Person addressed as 'Panditji' was of darkish complexion, well built and tall. He seemed very forceful and appeared to be the decision maker for the team.

'Guruji' seemed to be very wise, less aggressive, but confident, balanced and fully in control again.

I must ask Babulal about them.

I had lost faith in Gandhi as well as the Indian National Congress after the Non-Cooperation

Movement had failed. I was eager to do something for the country, but lack of exposure and awareness stood in my way.

Therefore, when Panditji and Guruji were asking questions, I was clueless. Perhaps my self respect stood in the way of accepting an alternative path easily.

Next day, I decided to meet Babulal and get a clearer picture about what was going on.

My mind was struck by a thought to try meeting Mukund, if he was in the college and take his advice if I should take a serious plunge into the freedom fight or forgo the idea.

Perhaps he could help me.

No sooner did I reach the college, then Babulal called me. He was waiting for me. 'Bagga, you have to come with me. They want to meet you again.'

This surprised me. I was a little anxious. Why again?

Obviously, there was no time left to discuss or share with Babulal about yesterday's happenings. Once again, I was taken to their hiding place, but it was not the same place today.

Besides, Guruji was replaced by someone else, called 'Avdhut'.

He was very lean and perhaps not as strong as Guruji, whom I had met yesterday. He was more confident, intelligent and sharp.

I assumed him to be having a final say in the selection of volunteers. There was another round of discussions for at least one and a half hour, before I was allowed to leave.

For a week, the discussions continued with either Panditji, Guruji, or Avdhutji. As a result, I had a lot of food for thought.

(It was only much later I came to know why they were given such names).

They talked about the current situations prevailing in the different states of India, and how I could involve myself in the mission. They also asked about my skills and how would I be useful in the work done by the group.

After several interactive sessions, interviews and interrogations with these leaders, there came a moment when I had to take the final decision.

It took me several sleepless nights, pondering over and considering all the pros and cons including both my life and that of my family, who were dependent on me.

Besides, I was still under Mukund's very strong Pro-British influence. Obviously, I found it more difficult to decide whether to join this revolutionary group or not.

But again, there has to be a life changing moment, sooner or later. There was no possibility of studying further or going back to the college for me now. Not with Banvari Bhaiya in the jail.

Besides, If I decided to fight against the British Government after completing my graduation, it would be too late.

It was not the deliberations with the interviewers that helped me change my mind, but their passion and steadfastness for the purpose, that impressed me the most.

After so many interviews and discussions, my mind was very clear. There was no time to be wasted now. The earlier I joined this group, better it was.

I had an opportunity to satiate my innermost passion. I ought to be the part of this revolutionary group. It was a God given chance and I should grab it. This had fallen into my lap on its own.

Once I decided to join the group, I also made another decision, and that was to leave the house. I do not know what triggered this feeling, but the more I thought about it, more convincingly it emerged. Staying at home, and participating in all these activities looked unfeasible to me.

I accepted that it was not an easy decision to leave the house so impulsively.

Especially after Banvari Bhaiya was jailed, to run away from the responsibilities would not be a wise step. The burden of guilt was too heavy for me to carry. On the other hand, if I did not take this decision now, there was no possibility of getting him released without the team's support.

Everything will fall in place soon, I told myself. The next day, as was decided, I was to give my final reply by 11 O'clock in the morning, I went to meet them.

Let me clear one myth here.

There were many legends who had pledged themselves to such secret societies. But one had neither to sign any pledge in blood in the presence of the goddess Kali, nor had to hold a forefinger over burning lamp as a test, or take a verbal oath, but a lot of caution was observed about planning the meetings. Interestingly, every time our meeting place used to change.

The meetings were held sometimes at a temple, or a small school, or at someone's house, terrace etc. They were held in complete secret. A safe route was followed each time, to avoid any suspicion by the British Police. And the message for the meeting venue was either conveyed by Babulal, Lalaji or his assistant.

Today I was to meet them at a gymnasium (Akhada).

Guruji and Avdhutji were waiting for me. They were always in time, and fully attentive to what I wanted to ask or speak.

"Namaste Guruji! Namaste Avdhutji!", I greeted them and both nodded in appreciation.

"So what have you decided? We do not have much time now."

"Yes, Guruji. I feel privileged to work under you. Working under your guidance, for the freedom of our country."

As soon as I said this, Guruji got up from the settee and hugged me. So much affection!

Avdhutji followed suit, and hugged me.

Nothing more was spoken. I was told that I would be informed whenever anything came up. I was never formally told that from that very moment I was to consider myself a member of the revolutionary party. Besides, one was not expected to spend much time being in the group, but there was always something to learn when we were with the leaders.

I thought that it was important to confide in them about Banvari Bhaiya.

"Guruji, my brother Banvari is arrested. I am eager to get him out of the jail."

Guruji was already aware of it. "Yes, we are trying to get the boys released soon."

Gradually I came to know about the other young men of my acquaintance who had similarly been won over. I was taken aback to learn that Banvari Bhaiya had already joined this group long ago.

Once I learnt this fact, a lot of things became clear to me.

Banvari Bhaiya's activities, interests, secret meetings and his readiness to meet some of his friends. It was this revolutionary group that he was connected with all along.

I felt very emotional. It was an overwhelming moment for me to realise that Banvari Bhaiya had not told me about this. I think he still thought me to be a small boy. Initially, I was little hurt, but eventually I was very proud of my brother.

I learnt later that 'Panditji' was none other than Pandit Ramprasad Bismil 'Bismil da', and 'Guruji' was Manmathnath Gupta.

'Avdhutji' was the great Rajendranath Lahiri. These were the key persons of the revolutionary group in Northern India.

There was a special reason why each leader, or even a volunteer was called with a spiritual name, which will be disclosed later.

There was a striking characteristic of all three of them, and it was their dedication and readiness to do anything for India's freedom. I considered myself fortunate to be working under them.

There were many others in the group, but as far as possible, all the group members rarely came in contact with each other.

> *It was mandatory to be aware of the regular developments at the national level to get seriously involved in the activities of the group.*

On the Eastern front, Calcutta was a major centre for the revolutionary parties.

Preparations of the bombs and getting the weapons from foreign countries was the prime mission in Bengal. Calcutta being a harbour, it was natural and easy for the revolutionaries to make contacts with the foreign agencies. The flame of the freedom was burning there all the time. Since it was the British capital initially, the scars and the impact of the war of 1857 between the Indians and the British still haunted the memories of people there.

The power of the freedom fighters, who were fearless and never hesitated in facing the British Police, was evident all over India.

There were strong and dedicated groups who had vowed to sacrifice their lives for the country.

In Northern India, there were many cities where the revolutionary activities were carried out successfully right under the nose of British Police. New volunteers continued to join the group. The revolutionaries gathered from bigger as well as smaller cities. Ultimate places of action were the famous four i.e., Lucknow, Agra, Allahabad and Delhi.

I soon learnt that there were at least two to three major revolutionary groups operating from Lucknow itself.

Since, I had left home now, and was spending a lot of time with the team leaders, they had started involving me in various activities of the groups.

This was not easy to start with. For a person like me who had lived comfortably in a family, a sudden change in the life style, complete dependence on the team-mates, or their families who provided food and shelter, besides to carry out orders of the leaders was completely a new experience for me.

Nonetheless, I was determined to go ahead with this, and there was no possibility of returning now.

I learnt that many volunteers had left their homes like me. We stayed together, shared whatever food was available, or starved at times and slept in places not suitable enough. My determination helped me to get over all these difficulties and focus on being part of the team to the best of my abilities.

The team leaders tested me on various occasions for my reliability and faithfulness which I seemed to clear successfully.

Since for me, it was the question of life and death to survive in the team.

My positive attitude alongwith the goodwill created by Banvari Bhaiya helped me to create an image of a dependable team member soon.

Gradually, I was a confidante to some of the leaders, especially Rajendra Lahiri and Pandit Ramprasad Bismil. It was interesting to learn their individual ways of approaching any issue, problem or situation.

Lahiri suggested to Bismil da that since forces of the revolutionaries were scattered, no constructive outcome could result in spite of such hard work by the teams. Why not merge all the small parties into one and create a strong - All India team?

This idea was circulated to all the centres for their opinion and advice, mainly in the Northern India. The discussions were carried out in different centres, and this suggestion was welcomed by everyone and everywhere, that a single party should come into existence.

In fact, we were pleasantly surprised to learn that the revolutionaries from different cities like Calcutta, Delhi, Allahabad, Kanpur, Benaras had also been working upon the same idea for some time.

A single party by the name of 'Hindustan Republican Association' was formed soon.

This name was given by the great Shachindranath Sanyal, writer of the ' Bandi Jeevan.' He was also a scholar, writer and an orator of a very high calibre. He was the senior most, and commanded great respect from the group.

He at once gave the amalgamated party not only a name, but also wrote its constitution and gave it a revolutionary status.

His very name was a certainty of the integrity for the party.

The constitution of our party was then charted out, mainly by the two scholars Shachindranath Sanyal and Ganesh Shankar Vidyarthi. Vidyarthi was a journalist, a dedicated team member and more of an expert in such matters.

Thus, the people with simplicity and high values in our team were able to create a history for the revolutionary party. Eventually, a constitution was formed by their efforts and its printed copy was shown to all of us in a meeting.

Only five of us were present in the meeting that day in a small village school. Ramprasad Bismil, Rajendranath Lahiri, Ashfaq Ulla Khan, Manmathnath Gupta and myself.

Ashfaq- Ulla Khan was a close associate and more of a disciple of Bismil da. He was as strong as Bismil da but remained quiet most of the time, and appeared more like a thinker. He was a very reliable and wise member of our team.

Manmathnath had collected the final printed copy from Vidyarthi. I was fortunate to have accompanied him for this task. "Guruji, the final print of the constituition is ready." When he reported, all of us were eager to see it. I was very excited too.

The Constitution was printed on a thin, yellow paper.

There was a spark in his eyes. All of us were overjoyed to see the constitution of the 'Hindustan Republican Association'. The vision of our party was taking shape finally.

Ashfaq Ulla Khan got up from his settee and took the constitution paper to study in the dim light of the room. 'Avdhutji, this is very precise and good!'

Bismil da exclaimed, "Yeh kya? Peela kagaz? Ye to peela hi hai." (What is this? A yellow paper? This paper is yellow.)

Everyone eagerly started reading and discussing the Constitution. After a long discussion, we started referring to it as the 'Peela Kagaz' or 'Yellow Paper', and that's how it came to be known to all of us.

Eventually, the constitution was known as the Yellow Paper in the history of HRA, the short form of the 'Hindustan Republican Association.'

Let me share some information on how the constitution was written, or about its contents.

The 'Hindustan Republican Association's' ultimate objective was to form the United States of India.

The constitution did not use the word 'Socialism' anywhere, nor did it talk of class struggle. Perhaps that idea of freedom was the only thing that mattered to all the party members at that moment, and perhaps the meaning of the socialism was not too clear to them to put it on the paper.

It carried powerful thoughts which were appropriate for those times. All the seniors readily accepted it. Funds and arms for the objectives were to be procured through the voluntary as well as forced contributions.

One should not forget that this constitution was prepared when there existed no actual parties in India. The HRA was the first Indian party which had envisaged a society where exploitation of man by man had to be eradicated.

Sanyal was a sincere believer of the spiritual values as preached by the Indian saints and seers. He refused to entertain the idea even for a moment that the high-sounding philosophy about brotherhood was only a cloak to conceal the real nature of things going on inside the society. This was certainly a strong thought, which was needed for our organisation to survive and carry out the missions that required sincerity and complete devotion towards the purpose.

I wondered what would have happened if this had been the basis of the constitution of free India, and how successful it could have been.

Once this was done, a series of preparations were on the way. New members were added to the party after a strict scrutiny about their whereabouts and the family connections. And once a member was enrolled, it was mandatory for him to keep his membership secret both from the public and the police.

The labourers and peasants who worked as helpers needed to be organised by the party. The constitution had a very strict approach towards this. According to it, the deviated member was not only to be expelled but might also be sentenced to death.

However, the arms were made available to every member provided the funds were adequate to take care of all, or enough supplies were received from some resources.

The number of the new recruits was growing rapidly. It is difficult to mention the name of all those who had joined the 'HRA' under the able leadership of Pandit Ramprasad Bismil, Rajendra Lahiri and under the perfect guidance of Sanyal and Vidyarthi.

Often, nobody knew who the team-mates were in our team, until and unless we gathered for a mission.

One of the most popular new entrants was Chandra Shekhar Azad, whose fearless approach and bravery won the hearts of all the team members.

He had a clear vision of what could be done to be noticed by the Government. He could convince the leaders as well as the volunteers to carry out his orders.

However, his greatest quality was to assume different roles and act, where no police could ever identify him.

My experiences were different while joining the party. I used to imagine that I should be ready to die as I was courting the death. Later, with the practical experiences, I learnt that it was certainly dangerous to get involved in the activities of the group, but not that dangerous in comparison to the happiness of the freedom it would bring to us after all.

I started to get accustomed as the time passed. One does become strong and fearless in missions like this.

We soon realised that to carry out various activities of the 'HRA,' the first priority was money. It was needed for the upkeep of the revolutionaries, as well as for other important expenses of the party.

The travel of the emissaries entailed a good deal of money. The messengers had to be sent for important communications, notwithstanding the fact that all the letters were censored.

The books and the pamphlets bought or published by the party involved a lot of money too. The biggest expense was of course the purchase of the arms through national and inetrnational smugglers. As there was no war going on now, we could not expect donations for the time being.

Where would it come from? Money raised from the subscription received from the members was barely sufficient to buy even the books. There were some sympathisers who contributed a large sum to the party, but still that was not enough.

In Lucknow, Agarwalji was a big support to the revolutionaries, Babu Shivprasad Gupta in Benaras and few other generous donors who made big contributions. The amount would be as high as 500 rupees every now and then, without asking for a receipt. They had a great faith in our leaders like Sanyal, Bismil da and others.

It was not fair to depend entirely on their donations and resources.

Our party was growing fast in strength as far as the organisation was concerned. However, the lack of money was paralysing its progress. It was decided that our FC department (Forced Contribution) needed to become active.

Forced contribution was the method adopted by the revolutionaries of Bengal long ago. There were many countries who had adopted this method during their time of crisis.

The forced contribution in plain English means robbing, but with a purpose, such as the killing in the wars is done with a purpose.

I did not like the phrase 'Forced Contribution'. It seemed to be too far from the reality, but on the whole conveyed the meaning correctly.

> *Frankly speaking this department was considered a necessary evil. This was the only option left as the arteries of the party had started stiffening without sufficient funds. That is what the leaders of the 'HRA' felt.*

There was always a possibility of being questioned as to why we were doing these activities.

Often the boys were from the families who were more into education, and their fathers were either working for the British Government, or having some small business. Naturally, it was not expected of their children, to loot the people. However, as I had learnt the hard way, this was not a drawing room politics, but a hard-core war with the King, and the fight had to go on till the end.

One of the immensely experienced leaders for such an adventure was Jogesh Chaterjee, so responsibility of leading the first village hold up was given to him. It was the first attempt for me as well. Everyone was very optimistic about it, but as the luck would have it, it turned out to be a disaster.

Initially, the leaders had carried out a detailed survey and evaluation of the whole conspiracy was done very secretly and with no one having any information about it.

I too was informed later, that I was supposed to participate in this village hold up.

A sense of thrill took me over as I learnt about it.

The village chosen for the hold up was in the Fatehpur district. A volunteer named Ravindra accompanied me. We were both instructed to board a train to Mugalsarai and then onwards to Khaga railway station.

We did not have the slightest idea about what would happen when we reach Khaga. As the time passed, I realised that I was not at all prepared for this type of expedition. I had anticipated to manage some administrative work when I had joined the party.

However, unlike the theoretical divisions in other offices, the departments did not exist in the party. Originally, it was proposed to keep two separate departments, namely the 'Civil' and 'Military'. Eventually everyone was designated with the duty to play multiple roles. And so, for the time being, we were a part of the 'FC' party. Sometimes we had an impression (being inexperienced) that we were selected to die for the freedom of our country, and it was time now.

We were given 48 hours' time, during which we had to make our veprations.

Funnily, the excitement took us to watch a movie, as if this was the last time such a pleasure was available to us.

I tried to complete my half-written articles in the remaining time, which I used to send to various magazines. I posted them thinking that these were my last articles.

Ravindra was excited like me, but in a funny way. He started singing songs of Rabindranath Tagore, depicting death with the fervour of love and devotion.

As we were boarding the train to Mughalsarai, I told Ravindra, 'We are committing such a lowly crime for our country's independence. Is it justified?' Ravindra nodded.

Perhaps all the revolutionaries who were joining us would think about it at some point of time, I am certain. The revolutionaries were converging from the different parts of the province for this mission, and as we descended at the station after a long journey, a familiar and smiling face welcomed us. We were asked to follow him silently.

We walked for miles and miles without asking any questions.The other team members were following their leader in the same manner, which we came to know afterwards. We were not familiar with the destination, or the roads and the detours that we undertook.

At that time dacoities were frequent in this region, so a force named the 'Special Police Guard' had been created to deal with the dacoits. Coincidentally, the guards too were deputed on the same road that we had taken, so we had to be extra cautious. It did not threaten our lives though, as the thud of their boots could be heard even from a mile.

It dawned upon me that we were not marching actually towards our death, but towards learning via experience in the 'Forced Contribution'.

Finally, in the cover of the darkness of the night, we reached near a mango tree, where we were ordered to halt. We went inside the dense mango grove and opened the packages, that is what others had brought along. Out came the pistols and the revolvers, from the folded beddings and simple shoulder bags.

The action was on. Jogesh Chaterjee, being the leader of the mission, counted the arms and distributed among ten of us.

He also had outlined what would be the duty of each man and how and where would he have to take position.

We were supposed to look like regular dacoits, for which all of us wore a turban, the long hanging end of which was used to conceal our faces.

All this was done quickly, within a few minutes. The smallest detail like wearing the right shoes was also checked, so that the whole operation went flawlessly and with a professional touch.

The extra luggage was hidden in the grove, to be collected when we return. We carried only two rifles, revolvers, pistols and a Nepalese *khukri* along. There was no firearm left for me, so I was given a short sword. I was not very excited about it.

We were asked to avoid speaking in English, and intersperse our words with plenty of abuses and also to address each other as hawaldar as the dacoits did.

The British Indian police took dacoity for granted. Whereas if they knew that we were a group of the armed revolutionaries, they would not sleep until they annihilated us.

A strange and unexpected thing happened just then. As we were about to start, suddenly there was a loud sound of a gun-shot.

Completely flabbergasted, we lay flat on the ground as taught.

Within minutes, we heard the footsteps of a man, and we all became alert. Much to our relief, he turned out to be the man of our own group.

Our leader got up abruptly and asked sternly what the matter was.

The man was very nervous. He apologetically said that his revolver had gone off suddenly, and apologised again. We all realised that our team member had pulled the trigger off due to excitement and lack of knowledge about revolvers.

There was relief as well as some disappointment due to this mistake.

On the other hand, the village seemed to come alive, and men with the lanterns started moving here and there. It was evident that the suspicion of the villagers had been aroused by a revolver shot.

We had planned to attack a moneylender's house in this village, but now it was certain that now alerted servants of the moneylender would be ready with the guns. The prospect of the success of our plan had been completely blasted off due to a small unintentional yet irresponsible act.

Naturally, the state of commotion in the village would not subside now for some hours. It was clear that our plan had failed.

As a result, the leader decided to call off the plan.

The action for which we had burnt midnight oil for several days, and the success was a certainty, had to be called off. Unfortunately, this was the only right course under the circumstances.

Of course, our team mate was deeply guilty. His revolver was taken away instantly and he was to be expelled eventually. However, we all felt sorry for him.

We returned safely, with a good lesson learnt, but poorer by few hundred rupees, which would have helped us make the team stronger. After this incident, the things did not go very smoothly for our group for some time.

In the meanwhile, we came to know that one of the revolutionaries, Gopi Mohan Saha had killed an English man in Calcutta, when he tried to assassinate Charles Tegart, the head of the Detective Department of Calcutta Police, who was leading the fight against revolutionaries.

This had resulted in the arrest of hundreds of youths all over the country, especially in North India and Calcutta. This sadly, included Jogesh Chatterjee also.

The 'Hindustan Republican Association' decided to remain in low profile for some time. Consequently, leadership of the 'FC' department, our group was given to Ramprasad Bismil, who was a great leader and everyone accepted him as the leader without any question.

As the term the 'Forced Contribution' was pretty unwieldy and 'Dacoity' did not appear suitable, we were looking for a password or expression, which would mean nothing when a stranger or unwanted person heard it, at the same time, our team could convey the inherent message across.

Once when our scheme was nearing success, someone cried out "GYAN JO HAI, SO BARIBANDA HAI", which meant that KNOWLEDGE HAS PETERED OUT.

The 'Gyan' became a synonym for the 'Forced Contribution' and a man taking part in the mission was the 'Gyani,' i.e., the one who has attained the spiritual knowledge.

Further the manipulation round the nucleus of the word got a whole new set of words, basically related to the spiritual attainment at various levels.

Eventually, we evolved a vocabulary with its help as the central theme, and the derived names were already in circulation for some time now. It was easier to code our names, and a new language emerged as a result.

Words like 'Guruji', 'Panditji' and 'Avdhutji' were already in use, so that now a full-fledged language system was established to address some team member, depending upon his status in the party.

The old and senior Gyanis were called the 'Avdhut' who had participated in more than four hold ups, and the leader was named the 'Paramhansa.'

Thus after Jogesh Chatterjee, Ramprasad Bismil was the new 'Paramhansa.'

The 'Avdhuts' were restricted only to eight in number per province as the members were now too many in numbers.

At the same time, those who were absconding were known as the 'Jivanmukta,' meaning 'emancipated' though alive.

This meant that the spiritual expression was used more to convey to each other about the plans or the group mates, rather than its actual meaning.

This was very convenient, and all of us started using it freely without any fear of being followed by a stranger or a CID.

After Bismil da became our new 'Paramhansa,' we were successful in carrying out a few hold ups, despite his weak organising skills.

Soon a development took place, which changed the course of history for the revolutionaries of the 'HRA' party.

It was in fact, a brain child of Panditji - Ramprasad Bismil himself, who was certain about the success of the plan, but which had very deep repercussions, affecting one and all connected with the scheme in due course.

❑

3

The Indian Railways Job

Mukund Narrates

It was really shocking. I was looking for Satish and Banvari in the college, instead I came across a locked and sealed library. I stood motionless for a few minutes, desperately trying to understand what could have actually happened.

After a few moments, I heard some voices. There was a group of students passing by the adjacent corridor. I could recognise one of them. He was Bansi Nath, a student from our batch.

When he saw me waiting at the library door, he came briskly towards me and whispered, 'Go away from here. All are arrested.' and rushed back, lest anyone found him out there.

His fear prevented him from saying anything further, which astounded me.

Did he mean that Satish and Banvari were arrested?

A feeling of guilt took over me. If only I had stayed back that day and pacified Bagga, he and Banvari could have been saved from this plight.

Coming back to the reality, I realised that it was wiser for me to get away from the library as soon as possible. But what about Bagga and Banvari? How to find out about their whereabouts?

It would be unsafe to visit their house immediately. What if police are keeping a watch over there? Safety being my prime concern, I swiftly got away from there, and went out of the college as quickly as possible.

I almost ran while returning home, without looking to my left or right. Today the road seemed unending.

I was very much afraid as I was certain that the police might emerge from a remote corner anytime to question me regarding my connections with Bagga and Banvari.

Running and panting when I reached home, I saw Mataji sitting on the front corridor, coughing.

It was my usual practice to sit next to Mataji and chat with her on various topics starting from the household to the relatives when I returned home from the college.

Today, I just muttered, 'Namaste Mataji!' ('Hello Mother!') and went inside the house. Grabbing any book that I could lay my hands on, started reading to pretend as if I was busy studying.

After almost one and a half hour Mataji came in. She found me studying quietly. She was very surprised.

She asked me with a concern, "Sab theek tau hai beta?" (Is everything okay Son?)

I tried to feign being normal, "All is good, Ma. Do not worry. I was preparing for the exams. I would be there in the kitchen in some time and then we would have dinner together."

My mother, Ushadevi, suffered from the occasional fits due to asthma, therefore it was my routine to help her in the kitchen as well as other household chores. But today it was impossible for me to get over my fears and help her.

After some time when I went to the kitchen, Mataji had kept the dinner ready. She had sensed that there was something seriously wrong, and avoided asking me further questions.

Without any conversation with Mataji, I hurriedly had dinner and went off to sleep wishing that tomorrow would be a peaceful day.

The next two days passed in a dilemma, whether I should visit Bagga's house and find out what the situation was, or to let some more time pass.

It was impossible for me to imagine how panic-striken Uncle and Aunty would be if anything had happened to Bagga and Banvari. And what about Leela?

I continued to live with this dilemma for more than a week.

On one hand, our friendship compelled me to find out about the well being of Satish and Banvari and on the other hand, I wanted to keep away from the sharp eyes of the Lucknow police.

As a result, I continued studying at home and refrained from going to the college or getting in touch with Bagga or his family.

This was unlike me, as Satish and I used to meet at least twice a week, even during the college holidays.

Almost after a fortnight and in the early hours of the night, around 9:00 pm, there was a knock at the door.

A chill passed through my bones. The police had traced me after all.

Nervously I opened the door. Multiple thoughts crossed over my mind in a few seconds. How would I face Pitaji?

It was with much effort, I reached for the door, perspiring though it was not so hot being the early hours of the night.

To my great surprise it was Satish. Wasn't he jailed? Thank God! What a relief to see him!

How foolish of me not going to his house to inquire about him and Banvari! I pulled him inside the house and almost shouted, "Bagga! Where were you? What is going on?"

Satish smiled in his original unperturbed style and quietly sat on a sette in the room.

That was his usual place whenever he came to visit me, "Mukund! Banvari Bhaiya is arrested for distributing pamphlets against the Government at the Residency, and is jailed for three months."

He narrated in short about what had happened in the college library and the incidence of the pamphlet distribution. I stared at him speechlessly, feeling sorry for both the brothers, and obviously angry at their plunging directly against the British Police. It was a short-sighted revolutionary action. Luckily, Satish had survived from going to the jail.

"Bagga! Thank God you are out of it now. So let us get back to the college studies. The life gives one more chance to everyone, and this is it!"

Satish still had enough time to prepare for the exams, and to pass successfully. He was good in studies.

I was wrong, if I expected Satish to appear for the exams. "That is not possible. I have left the house, and am going to Benaras." Satish got up and announced.

"Why Benaras?" I was shocked.

Satish continued, "I can not tell you anything presently." "No! No!" I got up from my chair and came near Satish.

Putting my hand on his shoulder, I pleaded, "Bagga, we have College exams coming up in a fortnight. Why don't you appear for that? Within two years, you will complete your Graduation and that will be a good degree. The other things can wait."

Satish seemed irritated with my logic. "Mukund, what about Banvari Bhaiya in the jail? How can you call my fight as other things when each passing day is a delay in gaining freedom for our country?"

I struggled in vain to persuade him, "Think about your parents and Leela. Since Banvari is jailed, it is your responsibility to look after them. Uncle wants you to graduate and then start working."

Satish's reply was unexpected. "Mukund, I need your help in this. Promise me that you will take care of my parents and Leela in my absence."

His words reflecting faith in me, were unexpected. It paralysed me.

Satish paused to add, "Mukund, I want a personal favour from you."

Without waiting for my reply, he caught my hand and said, "Mukund! I propose for my sister. Will you marry Leela?"

This was so sudden that I was speechless and completely dumbfounded.

He hastily added, "There is not much time now. But you know the life-story of my two sisters. I do not want Leela's life to be ruined. I am certain that by marrying you, Leela will lead a very happy life."

Satish was getting into the series of foolish and eratic decisions and this one concerned me directly.

He continued to speak, "You can take time to decide. I will keep you informed about my whereabouts, but if things don't work out well, and anything happens to me, you can meet Lalaji Paanwala at the Chowk."

I was totally dazed. Satish was important to me, but so were my principles and dreams. I did not want to do anything that would go against the British Raj in India.

What about my future and my career?

My parents and I had toiled hard to reach here. And what about father's dream for me?

"Bagga! Please go home and talk to your parents before taking such a hasty decision. How shattered they will be to hear this?"

"No, Mukund! This is final. I have to perform my duty towards my country. Yes, you are free to take a decision about marrying Leela. Let me know when I come next time."

With these words, Satish hugged me. I did not realise when he opened the door and rushed out, as if melting away in the darkness.

Satish had left me in a lurch.

There is something about the people who make up their minds. Once they decide upon something, the Universe conspires to help them, and people around them are compelled to agree with their wish.

Satish had made up his mind, and it did not matter to him what the world had to say about it. I slumped in the chair. These were the life-defining moments for all of us.

The next morning, I went to Bagga's house. There was more clarity in my mind now and fears had taken a back seat. Nonetheless, I was at a loss about what I would convey to Uncle, Aunty and Leela!

It appeared that Uncle had already left for the office perhaps that is why the door was half open.

I entered the house without any sound, and as per my habit, went straight to the kitchen. Aunty was in the kitchen, cooking. Leela was there too.

Aunty raised her head from the stove, and exclaimed in one breath, "Aa gaya beta? (Welcome, son!) Do you know where is Bagga?"

Leela was looking at me. I could not understand her expressions. For the first time, I was embarrassed to look at her.

I evaded her look and went to the corner where Aunty was preparing rotis on a small stove (Sigari), "Chachi! Bagga might have gone for some work, and would return soon."

Kamala Aunty, a proficient cook and a poised woman, apparently remained undisturbed. Only while turning the rotis, her hand trembled a little, "I thought he might have informed you. I am much worried now that Banvari is also not around."

I could not disclose anything to her, try as I might. Was it a dilemma, or was I avoiding to see Aunty in pain? I tried to lie, "Satish was mentioning some work in the college library, perhaps he had to travel for that."

I pretended to look surprised at the mention of Banvari, "Where is Banvari?"

Leela looked at me and said, "He is caught and imprisoned by the British Police for 3 months."

She narrated to me in short about the unfortunate happenings with Banvari.

It was sad to see the two strong women suffering silently for the sake of their family, who in fact were out to sacrifice their lives for the country.

However, I tried to learn about Banvari's imprisonment, but from a distance, lest I would be expected to visit him in the jail.

It was difficult to face Leela. I wondered if she knew about Bagga.

Then I talked to Aunty about my mother's illness, and other general topics like the weather, food etc, to make the atmosphere lighter and normal.

After a short, meaningless visit to Bagga's house, I returned home. Though I wanted to tell them the truth, or at least give an idea or warn them, I was unsuccessful.

No information about Bagga could I share with Aunty or Leela.

It was unfair not to disclose that he had left home and joined the revolutionaries, as that would start a new series of worries in their mind, and frankly speaking, I wanted to avoid their questions on this issue.

I soon realised immensity of great responsibility that Satish had entrusted upon me.

In spite of it, I decided not to visit Banvari in the prison, at least for the time-being.

While returning home, I kept looking around if there was any police or detective following me. But there was nobody to be seen so conspicuous on the road.

Several passers-by were busy and indifferent, and a few bullock carts creaking their way on the muddy road, disturbed the atmosphere.

As I reached home, I decided to put the thoughts of Bagga, Leela and their family at the back of my mind till my exams got over, and focus completely on studies.

The days started to fly past, and I continued to study with full attention. When father saw me studying sincerely, he was very happy.

On the other hand, mother had sensed that something was seriously wrong between me and Bagga. She did not question me much since she was a person of few words. Perhaps she believed in waiting wisely till I would disclose it myself to her.

Few days prior to the exams, Mataji came to me in the early morning, "Mukund, Leela has come to see you."

I got up with a start. I had been studying till late hours during these days, shutting myself completely away from Bagga's family.

Why should Leela come home so early? However, I could not avoid her.

With drowsy eyes, I welcomed Leela.

Leela appeared to be agitated, "Mukundji," Leela exclaimed, "Father has sent me to ask if you have any news about Bagga Bhaiya or have you heard from him. He has not come home since so many days." It was apparent that she was trying to stop tears rolling down from her eyes.

She seemed to have grown up suddenly.

Leela added softly, "Please tell me the truth, has he fled with those baagis (revolutionaries)?" and started crying.

Things were not going to be easy for me in the future, I realised.

I consoled her, "Please don't cry Leela. I am not aware of anything. The last time I had met him was at your house. I do not know what he had decided after that." I continued to lie.

Leela was a strong girl, just as Satish's sister would be. It was sad to see her cry like this. I went near Leela, and sympathetically added, "Leela, he will return. He is competent and a brave boy. I will try my best to find his whereabouts."

Between her sobs, Leela said, "I know. Bhaiya did talk to me about this. But I could never imagine him taking this step." So Leela knew about Bagga's decision.

I looked at her with concern this time. She was plain in looks with a natural innocence. Not exactly beautiful in face, but also not bad to look at.

Should I say yes to Bagga? Not only to agree with Bagga's decision, but also to take care of Leela and their parents. I was always going to do that, marriage or no marriage with Leela.

I had to be loyal to my close friend Satish. I said to her, "Leela, please do not worry. I am here to help you, Uncle and Aunty."

Wiping her tears, Leela went out of the room to see my mother.

Mataji always enjoyed talking to Leela, and had a natural liking for her. She could console Leela with a lot more care and concern than me.

Leela left soon. For a moment, I wished that she had stayed on. I could have talked to her for a longer time.

Much to my surprise, Gupta Uncle, Satish's father came to meet me in the evening.

On second thoughts, this was expected. But I was jittery to face him. I had been in awe of him all along and looked upto him as a person with a touch of class - 'Khandani'.

But today looking at his helpless stance, I forgot everything and realised that I must comfort him first.

"Welcome Uncle! Please have a seat." Uncle was in no state of mind to sit and chat with me. Instead, he took me to a corner of the room and softly asked, "Mukund, is it true that Bagga has joined the revolutionaries? I have heard something like that."

He held my hand so tight that it was impossible to lie about his beloved son.

My throat choked. I nervously tried to break away from Uncle's hold, thinking desperately to make up a fake story, but words failed me. He understood.

My silence gave him the answer and he let go off my hand, as if letting go his son by that gesture.

Regaining composure after a few moments, he patted me on the back, and turned to leave without a single word. Coincidentally my father entered the house right at that moment.

Gupta and Pandey families were on cordial relations, and there was a formality of some sort especially between the senior family members.

When Pitaji saw Gupta Uncle coming to our house unannounced at this hour, he was very surprised.

In spite of the friendship between Bagga and myself, there was a marked difference in the values, background and standards of living of the two families.

Besides, Gupta Uncle held a higher designation at the same office where Pitaji worked. Obviously, it was not very normal for him to visit our house so informally.

Pitaji was curious to know what had happened. He warmly greeted Uncle, “Bhaisahab, Nice to see you. Please share a cup of tea with us.”

Gupta Uncle politely excused himself and said that he was in a hurry to reach home, and left in a shattered stance without further communication.

Pitaji found this strange. He asked me what the matter was.

I could not lie to him. Deep within, I was trying to prove myself to be an honest son. I told him about Satish’s disappearance, and Banvari being imprisoned. As expected, Pitaji showed his disapproval with a sarcastic smile.

His reaction made me nervous and I thanked my stars that I had nothing to do with Satish, Banvari and their activities.

This incident would put a full stop for me to interact with Satish’s family, at least till the exams got over.

Finally, the annual exams began, for which I was eagerly looking forward to.

As the exams progressed, a sense of confidence emerged within me, while fairing well in the papers one after the other.

However, college exams and all the surroundings reminded me of Bagga, and the chain of thoughts would often take charge of my mind.

Hence, during the long stretches of holidays between the two exam papers, I tried visiting Satish’s house once.

As I reached the royal house, the atmosphere looked grim and lifeless. I met Uncle, who pretended to read a newspaper when he saw me. However, when I greeted him, he was warm, but cautious and avoided the reference of Satish completely.

Aunty remained the same, loving and motherly with me.

When she saw me coming, she looked at me with sad eyes, tears peeping from the corners. She asked, "How are you, my son?"

I smiled and sat next to her, my conscience pricked me.

I joined them for a meal. Aunty and Uncle were aware about my exams, and asked me how things were. I answered their questions. We all were trying to appear composed and normal but realised that something was amiss. That was the unseen presence of Bagga and Banvari in the house.

Leela was helping Aunty in the kitchen, but seemed in no mood to talk to me. I avoided talking about the sensitive issues, and came out as soon as possible, heaving a sigh of relief.

Two days later was my last exam of Economics–part 2. Thankfully, I completed it without any disturbance from any corner.

The month of May was half past, and summer was at its peak. Like almost everywhere in India, the weather of Lucknow was getting warmer day by day.

But I was oblivious of the heat, reason being my good performance in the exams. Unaffected by the surroundings, and feeling jubilant, I was returning from the college, feeling free and happy.

However, unlike the days that we had spent together, now there was no one to talk to or to share stories. I badly missed him while walking the usual one kilometre distance, and on the last day at the college. But it was no use remembering the old times now.

Thankfully, I was also away from any freedom fight and its influence.

Suddenly, I saw a young boy coming towards me. He was almost running. Why should anyone run in such a hot weather? I watched him curiously as he approached me.

He had a small beard and wore a head gear, similar to that worn by the Sikh community in Punjab.

He smiled at me and said, "Are you Mukund, Satish's friend?"

I was trying to guess who he was. Satish's name had alarmed me. But he did not look like a policeman, so after a moment I replied in affirmative.

The boy was tall, well built, wearing a long cream shirt. The colour of his shirt spoke volumes about the type of life this boy might be leading. It had gathered dust, probably due to lot of running around. He wore a loose pyjama, men's usual clothing in the northern parts of the country. His good quality shoes were now tattered.

His shoulder bag was stuffed with papers, from which he took one out and gave it to me. "This is for you from your friend."

Before I could say anything, he sprinted away and disappeared at far end of the road.

I was dumbfounded. So far I had only heard about how the revolutionaries worked.

I folded the paper nervously and put it in my bag. I did not have courage to open and read it immediately.

I almost ran towards home, lest I would be caught by the police.

Much to my terror, I saw two policemen coming towards me. My heart missed a few beats.

I was nonplussed. "What if they asked me about my connections with Bagga and Banvari?" But no such thing happened. The policemen passed by casually without noticing me. I heaved a sigh of relief.

After reaching home, I went straight into my room, closed the door and locked it from inside, and eagerly opened my bag.

Mataji must have seen me entering the house. She knocked at the door, "Mukund, don't you want to eat lunch?"

I opened the door a little and replied breathlessly, "Ma, I shall come for lunch in five minutes."

Closing the door tightly, I opened the letter with shaking hands. It was written by Satish himself.

It read, "I am fine, and very happy. I have found the purpose of my life now. Please tell this to Pitaji and Mataji. The life is very different here though. I can not tell you about my whereabouts for security reasons. I know that you will take care of Leela and my parents. Vande Mataram!"

I read, and re-read the letter many times. For a moment felt my mind changing. What if…?

What If I sacrificed everything to be with Satish! But this was never going to happen. Since I knew that I could never do it.

I tore the paper carefully into small pieces and threw it away safely. Trying to calm my mind, I went to the kitchen and started telling Mataji about my exams.

Today she had prepared kheer for me, since she knew I really relished it.

Though I hardly took notice of it, and kept eating instead while talking to Mataji about the college, and how difficult the exam was.

She asked, "How did you like the kheer? I hope you enjoyed it, now that your exams are over."

I came out of my thoughts and replied hastily, "Yes, yes Mataji! It was very delicious. Sorry, I was preoccupied with my future plans."

Mataji casually asked, "So how was Bagga's exam? He did not come for solving difficulties this time."

This was the last thing I wanted to face under the circumstances, yet I decided to let Mataji know the truth.

"Ma, he did not appear for the exams. Hope Leela might have told you, he has left the house, very likely to join the freedom fighters' group."

It was necessary to break this news to Mataji, sooner or later.

Bagga was very dear to her and I knew that she would be shocked to learn this. But she did not say anything.

After the meal, I came out to sit in the front courtyard.

Now that the exams were over, I needed to brood over the events that had taken place in the last two months. Many decisions were waiting for me.

As far as marrying Leela was concerned, I had decided to go ahead for my friend's sake. That was the least I could do for the happiness of his family.

The more I thought about it, more I found myself to be fortunate.

Undoubtedly, Leela's family was considered higher in caste and carried a lot of goodwill in the society. Leela was a very good girl, and our families knew each other so well.

I must convey my answer to Bagga. But how to know his whereabouts and let him know about my decision? Should I meet Banvari in the prison? No, that would not be a right thing to do.

At that moment, I remembered Bagga mentioning about Lalaji Paanwala at the Chowk. I decided to meet him and find out everything.

The next day, I went to Lalaji's shop.

Lalaji welcomed me and smiled, "What brings you here, Mukund?"

I felt as if he had been expecting me. I tried to look composed and asked, "Lalaji! Hope everything is good?"

He answered, "Yes, All is good son."

I was at a loss now. Could I ask directly about Bagga? What if he was not aware of it? I was fumbling for some excuse, when I saw Agarwalji coming towards the shop.

He was one of the richest landlords of Lucknow. He came to the shop and said to Lalaji, "Make one good Benarasi paan for me."

Lalaji nodded. He made a paan for Agarwalji and while handing it over to him, pointed at me, "Saheb, this is Mukund, close friend of Satish."

Agarwalji half closed his eyes and studied me for a few moments. A shiver passed through my body. Then Agarwalji came near me, and whispered, "Your friend is fine. Do you want to send any message to him?"

My jaw dropped. Regaining my composure, I replied, "Yes,

Saheb! Please tell him that we all miss him. If he is thinking of returning..."

Agarwalji's attitude changed instantaneously. He said coldly, "I wonder if you are his friend at all," and left.

Lalaji picked up the thread. "Try to help your friend and his group. That is the least you can do."

I did not have any answer to this. It was futile to discuss about what was happening in my life currently.

I thought it best to leave from there.

Eventually, I started getting some information about the freedom struggle. There were numerous networks in the city and all over the country with many well wishers and supporters, who not only believed in the freedom fighters' mission and the revolutionaries but also supported them. It was difficult to find out who was a friend and who was not.

Such a turn of events made me stronger and reduced my fear of the British Police to some extent.

This also resulted in my visiting Bagga's house with less fear and more concern.

Initially, the visit used to be once a week, and then it increased to twice, and soon I started visiting them almost every alternate day.

This decision, and many other circumstances were to bring a great change in my life.

Many a times I would meet Gupta Uncle. His behaviour had changed considerably after Banvari was jailed and Satish had left the house.

He was no more the person who used to laugh and joke around. Instead, he was a shaky old man now who greeted back with a quiet nod.

Gupta Uncle must be visiting Banvari often in the jail, but I never had the courage to offer that I would join him, and he didn't ask also.

Sometimes, we exchanged a few sentences remembering Satish, but both knew that it was a dead end to our conversation. However, it used to bring life in Gupta Uncle's eyes for a few moments.

Aunty and Leela were always there to greet me. I perceived that they waited for my visits.

Leela was more vocal with me as the days passed. She would talk about her childhood days with brothers. She would remember sisters who were no more with her.

I had never given a thought to this before.

How a girl felt when she had lost two elder sisters and her brothers were involved in the revolutionary activities!

Whatever Banvari and Bagga's mission may be, their decisions had made Leela and her parents very helpless. I never favoured their ways.

It appeared that Bagga's parents had now given up on their sons' return.

During my frequent visits to Bagga's house, I would eat a paratha or kheer and share some jokes with Aunty, in whom I had noticed a remarkable change too.

Aunty tried her best to appear more composed and followed up on every information on the freedom struggle. Though she was not educated, she used to ask Leela, her husband and me about all the news related to the political scenario.

In fact, Aunty supported her sons for what they were doing, and secretly was also proud of it.

All these events compelled me to be updated about the recent happenings in the Indian politics. There used to be regular news in the newspapers and among people about the freedom movement.

Many Congress leaders addressed people on the issues of the freedom struggle, and changes regarding abandoning of the Non-Cooperation Movement.

Time and again the prominent leaders were jailed.

This gave rise to an upheveal among the masses, and riots against the British which was not only limited to the big cities like Calcutta or Delhi, but also spread to the smaller cities like Allahabad, Kanpur, Lucknow and villages, and had engulfed the whole nation.

A new party called the 'Swaraj Party', was created by a few Congress leaders like Motilal Nehru, C.R. Das, Subhash Chandra Bose, who all disagreed with Gandhi.

This party not only had a lot of money, but was also led by real intelligent and established leaders, to support their own ideologies and follow them. A lot of other leaders under the able leadership of Gandhi on the other hand, believed in tackling the situation through strategies, and not by violence.

As for the revolutionaries, the idea of giving a fight back to the King Emperor's men took back seat due to several reasons.

Firstly, they were recovering from the shock of abrupt calling off of the Non-Cooperation Movement, and were struggling to get hold of the situation. Many had given up their studies, families, home and had joined for the great purpose of freedom for the country. But ultimately, they remained outcaste and unwanted by any and every group working for India's freedom. No one openly supported them financially, let alone morally.

The revolutionaries were considered a restless and disoriented group of young boys, often addressed as terrorists, and people abstained from associating with them openly.

I found this very unfortunate. It was obvious that Satish and all those who were in the group of the revolutionaries must be passing through tough times, not to mention the situation Banvari was in, being imprisoned since long now.

While I was getting acquainted better with the real picture of Indian politics, late night one day, someone knocked at the door. I knew it was my friend Bagga.

Was he Bagga, or someone else? I could not recognise him for a moment. He had lost a lot of weight. He looked like a dacoit and had an apparent restlessness in his disposition.

Hurriedly, I got a glass of water for him which he hastily gulped down. Getting some more water for him, I asked with concern,

"Bagga, Are you okay?"

He looked pained, "Things are not good, Mukund. We are not getting support from anywhere."

Though it was not necessary for me to justify, I couldn't help mentioning, "Our Agarwalji?"

Before I could complete, Satish interrupted, "Only one Agarwal can not sustain our mission. A lot of money has to be pooled in. Our groupmates are starving."

"We have the courageous bunch of boys with us, who can gladly sacrifice their lives for the country. But the sad thing is, our ideology is not supported by any eminent leaders or big business houses."

I was proud of my freshly collected knowledge on this issue.

"Yes, I have heard about it. Gandhi is discouraging your work. How can one fight without a support? What will you do about the money? How do you manage everything?"

Satish, as warm as ever, patted on my back, "Mukund! You have never been like me. You are a sincere person. You will make your parents proud."

If anybody knows me so well, it has to be Bagga. My eyes filled with tears.

I went to the kitchen and fetched whatever food was available, in a plate for him. He took it happily, and started eating.

I said, "Bagga, why don't you approach the big leaders or the Indian entrepreneurs to help you? And why do you put yourself to so much struggle? Complete your studies and get a good job. You deserve a happy life."

All these words had no effect on Satish. He suddenly asked, "Mukund! What are your plans now? You will be a graduate by next month." I blushed. His concern made me feel guilty.

Gathering some courage I replied, "Yes, I will get my Graduation degree in two months. I had applied for a Railway job, if you remember. I have heard that Indian Railways is planning to recruit a lot of fresh graduates by September."

Satish, my magnanimous friend seemed happy for me.

There was complete silence for sometime. Both of us were thinking about the same thing, the decision of my marriage with his sister Leela.

I was at a loss for words. And we knew that it was time for him to depart.

I told Satish as a parting note, “Bagga, I am ready, I will.” Hearing my words, Satish jumped with joy and hugged me,

“I knew, my friend! I knew it! I am so happy. Congratulations! I am the happiest brother in the world.”

He appeared overwhelmed and was unable to express his joy! He sat for a moment, then started pacing the room, then held my hand, and thanked me again.

Talking about his sister’s marriage had exposed a very emotional side of Bagga, and he was his old self for a few moments.

I invited him to the marriage, “Please come for our marriage. It will be incomplete without you.”

However, both of us knew that it was only a wishful thinking.

Suddenly Satish looked much at peace, “Mukund! So far there is no Police record against me. But the British Government is very vigilant. They are keeping the track of all the freedom fighters- especially those like us. So I do not know when do we meet again.”

With these words, Bagga jumped out of the window and disappeared as he always did.

I staggered, thinking about my decision. With a mixed feelings of happiness, fear and worry, I could not sleep for many hours.

After this incident I did not see Satish for a long time.

In the meanwhile, final B.A. reults were declared by the University of Lucknow. I had passed the exams securing 53% marks. My joy knew no bounds. Everyone congratulated me for scoring such good marks with major subjects like Economics and Politics. I was happy to make my parents proud.

Many relatives came home to congratulate me. I was ecstatic. My dream to get a Government job was not very far from being fulfilled now.

A week after the results were out, Leela's parents came to meet us.

> *Bagga's family was held in great respect by the Lucknow social circles, my parents were delighted when they proposed for Leela to marry me.*

Naturally, there were other reasons which made them decide on me as their son-in-law, but I knew it well that the word had been put through by none other than Bagga himself.

An informal announcement was made about the engagement and soon everyone knew about my proposed marriage to Leela.

I missed Bagga and Banvari all along, to share the happy moments. Our parents were considering the marriage to take place either in October or November.

Nonetheless, I felt this was too early. I wanted to wait till I secured a stable job, not necessarily with the Indian Railways, but with any good company.

I was simultaneously staying updated to get more information on Indian Railways' work system.

Lucknow was an important Railway station in the Union Provinces, and interestingly, a new railway station was under construction, which I thought of visitng and reached the construction site.

As I reached the site, I stood amazed. It was a herculian project, and there were hundreds of labourers working incessantly to bring it to completion. This huge Railway Station was soon going to be reconstructed. I was completely awestruck to see its grand structure and the far-sightedness of the British Government.

The project was so imposing that the approval for this building was sought from the Viceroy himself. He was known to take personal interest in each new development of the Indian Railways.

The British Government had invited the famous architect, Mr. Zecob from London to build it. The Railway Station was in final stage of completion. I considered myself fortunate to witness this, admiring its architecture and the building.

Only if I get a job with Indian Railways, it would be like a dream coming true!

How I wished to make the best of both the worlds – job and then marriage.

Incidentally, I received a letter inviting me for an interview from the Indian Railways in January, 1923.

The letter had a list of instructions and conditions. They had mentioned that my interview would be held in a month's time. I started gathering more information about the Indian Railways, and the companies associated with it in India as well as United Kingdom. I did not want to lose this opportunity at any cost.

My studious and analytical nature helped me prepare well for the interview, and soon I received another letter for which I was waiting desperately. It was asking me to be present at the Lucknow Railways Office at the old Railway staion for the interview.

I could feel a new life waiting to welcome me. Soon the D-day i.e., day of my interview arrived.

I entered the Railways Office, it was a large room where a group of officers – about six of them- were seated. Out of the six, two were British and the other Indians. It seemed that they knew my background fully well and as they waved to me to sit on the chair facing them, I could sense a verbal attack to be inflicted upon me.

The questions regarding my education and background were bombarded at me. Shaking internally, I started replying to them – keeping in mind my father's faith in the British Government. This worked as a manifestation of the confidence for me.

I kept on reminding myself that this job was meant for me, and strangely, it was turning out to be exactly the same way.

All the interviewers appreciated my efforts to pass B.A. exams with a decent score and that too at first attempt, in spite of my modest background.

When I was asked how long I plan to stay in Lucknow, I excitedly informed them, that I was getting married soon, and looked forward to a settled life here.

This was well appreciated, and perhaps helped the interviewers to take the final decision, I guessed. The last question was shot at me, 'There are a lot of anti-Government activities going on in the United Provinces. Hope you are not related to any of the revolutionaries of Lucknow?'

I was stunned. This was completely unexpected.

I firmly replied, 'Of course not, Sir! I am a faithful servant of the British Government and will remain so all my life.'

Something within me died at that very moment. I knew that I was certain to get this job. But the excitement had waned off somehow.

Soon I received a letter from the Indian Railways. I was selected for the job - The prestigious, Indian Railways job as a clerk.

In two days as I received the confirmation letter from the Indian Railways' Administrative Department, I gathered courage to visit Lalaji's paan shop. I wanted to convey the news of my getting a job to Bagga.

I could sense sarcasm in Lalaji's stare. Instead, he said,

"Welcome, son! Seeing you after a long time. I hope you are happy in the British India?"

I was searching for an answer.

Lalaji continued, "It happens Mukund. People and friends meet and depart. However, Congratulations! Heard about your marriage. You are getting married to Satish's sister?"

I replied evasively, "Thank you! You have already got the news."

I wanted to ask Lalaji about developments in the freedom struggle and about the revolutionaries especially Satish. I wanted to convey to Bagga, that I have got the job finally.

But I felt let down by my own self and could wait no longer at the paan shop, I returned home soon.

That evening Leela came to see me. In fact, now that our engagement was announced, she visited my house less often and not so freely. Hence there must be something important today, Ithought.

Today she looked happy, after a long time since Banvari's imprisonment and Bagga's leaving the house.

She met Mataji first then she came to meet me. I was sitting in the front corridor. She sat next to me.

It was very easy to talk to her, knowing her now for many years. We had started talking about our future plans. In fact, I wanted to tell her all about my dreams, and ambitions whenever we met alone.

Leela congratulated me, "Aap ko naukri mil gayi."(You got the job.)

I nodded. She looked at me. She could guess that something was not right with me.

Leela held my hand and asked, "Why are you so quiet today? We will have a happy family life, and now you have such a prestigious job too."

I pulled my hand away and stood up. I hated myself today, the conversation with Lalaji had left some scars on my mind. In addition, Leela reminded me of her brother Bagga.

However hard Leela tried to talk to me about our happy future, marriage plans, and celebrations, it did not help me feel better.

So many emotions had taken charge of me in such a way, that in spite of a rosy future awaiting us, guilt and burden of not being a faithful friend to Bagga was crushing me down.

Leela found it futile to talk to me, hence without further conversation, she left.

Soon the time came for me to join my new job. It was August, 1923 and I was now an official employee of the Indian Railways.

Mataji and Pitaji were very proud of me and I in turn was very happy. The morning saw Mataji prepare a sweet as I would begin my job today and Pitaji came to drop me at the office. Whole day passed very happily, with me getting to know the other employees at the office, and interacting with some newcomers like me.

There were a few new employees like me, which made the working enjoyable, as most of us either were freshers, or with little work experience at a smaller organisation.

The day got over, another started, and it went on. Fortunately, other employees at the office were welcoming me and also very supportive in helping me settle in my work, gradually I got a grip on my work and surroundings.

It took me a while to adjust myself with the work, but after a few days, I could fit myself in the routine well. I used to reach the office in time and worked with complete sincerity.

We had a very strict boss, Shri Guha Ji. My mission was to keep him happy with my performance.

Lucknow was a big railway station in the United Provinces, after New Delhi. It was a junction for various Railways' routes in the Northern India. In fact, many trains used to connect the northern and the eastern parts of India through Lucknow. This made the office work growing all the time, and lot of new developments kept the staff busy with work and enthusiasm.

Eventually, the Railways Office staff too was expanded. The majority of the staff was shifted to a bigger office, which was a larger building. In fact, it was an old Haweli, owned by a merchant, and later confiscated by the Government when he passed away.

Leela's parents were keeping a good watch over me, now that I had secured the Railways job and was settling down well. In no time, as I started the job, they sent a message regarding the finalisation of our marriage.

Since so much time had already elapsed after our engagement, I had no reason to delay it any further, and neither did my parents. In a very short time, both the families were busy organising and preparing for the marriage functions.

Leela and her parents had accepted me in their family with warmth and enthusiasm. I was their son-in-law and, in a way, represented their sons (Satish and Banvari) in their absence.

My family was often invited to their house for meals, and showered with gifts. How I loved those days!

When I received my first pay, I was ecstatic! The confidence of achievement in life made me more and more strong to face the world proudly. I was earning good, and gradually my life began to give me all the worldly pleasures that one could only dream of.

On the other hand, I had stopped visiting Lalaji's paan shop, and avoided meeting him or Agarwalji. By no means did I want to connect myself with the revolutionaries who were blacklisted by our honoured Britishers. It could affect my career adversely.

The day of my marriage was approaching and there was excitement in the air. Though Leela's family could not afford a pompous celebration, they were all set to make it enjoyable and decorous.

After office hours, I would meet Mataji in the market for shopping, buying clothes and ornaments for Leela, and our family. It gave me immense satisfaction that I had the spending power now, to be able to afford a lot of things.

It was important for me to meet Guha Ji andrequest him for leave from the office for my marriage. Besides being a strict boss, he was also a proficient officer, known for his disciplined approach in everything.

Since I was still on a probation for the first six months, it was not easy for me to submit my leave application.

On a Friday evening after office hours, I knocked on Guha Ji's office door.

A steel voice from inside spoke unwelcomingly, 'Come in.'

I was trembling when I opened the door and entered his cabin. He looked at me questioningly.

I said hesitatingly, 'Namaste Saheb! I have come to invite you for my marriage.'

There was no obvious response.

I continued, 'Saheb, I am getting married on the 26th of October.' If I expected the words of congratulations or greetings from him, then I was mistaken. Guha Ji was more British than the real British, of whom I was afraid all along.

He questioned, 'How many days' leave are you asking for? And from when?'

I fumbled as he was reading my mind.

'Saheb! I thought if I get 15 days' leave then I can be of help to my parents and look after the guests and meet relatives who arrive.'

His reaction took me completely by surpirse. 'Okay Pandey! I am granting 15 days' leave to you without pay. But make sure that you resume office on the 16th day.'

Then he added in a quiet tone, 'There are a lot of changes coming in the accounting system of the Indian Railways. I want you to take up that as a part of your assignment when you resume after your marriage.

This was unbelievable! On one hand, I was allowed the full leave as required, and secondly, my boss appeared to be happy with my work that he was considering me to be given a specific responsibility.

I folded my hands and bowing to Guha Ji mumbled, 'Thank you, Saheb! I will be back in time.'

My happiness knew no bounds that day.

As soon as the office timings were over, I practically ran to Leela's house, to give her khushkhabari (good news) of the long leave granted to me from the office.

And then the days flew like a dream sequence. Finally bringing the most important day of my life – the day of my marriage.

I kept on telling myself that I was fortunate to marry a nice girl like Leela and thankful for the wonderful turn that my life was taking!

Many of our relatives had travelled from the distant as well as nearby towns visitng specially to attend the marriage ceremony.

Everyone was happy, and celebrations had started, even at Leela's house.

In spite of their two sons being away from the house, which must be very difficult, Leela's parents tried to welcome all our relatives smilingly, and did not let their pains be known to anyone. They had spent extravagantly on the preparations, which was evident from the preparations made for every event.

Many of our relatives told my parents that their son was very fortunate to get a girl from such a good family as a wife. This made Mataji and Pitaji really proud, and me very pleased.

The functions and the ceremonies of the marriage had begun, and I could hardly register what was happening around me.

On one hand, I was missing Bagga and Banvari's presence, but at a deeper level, I was relieved since I wanted the functions to get over without any disturbance or trouble.

As the ceremonies were coming to completion, Leela and I had to walk around the fire (perform wedding rings), where as per the custom, bride's brother is required to be present.

As the pujari (Hindu priest), called out for the bride's brother, we were taken aback and were speechless.

It was very unfortunate that none of Leela's two brothers could remain present at Leela's marriage for this ceremony. I tried to pacify Leela by saying that it was destiny, where one is helpless and can not do anything.

To add to the problem, in a few moments, we saw a policeman entering the marriage hall hurriedly.

He had a large wooden baton in his hand, and had the appearancee of a ruthless officer. I was nonplussed. This was very horrifying.

Before anyone could react to a policeman's entry in the middle of our marriage function, he came straight towards us. The British Police had finally found out my connection with Satish.

The policeman did not stop there. He approached the marriage ceremony area and put aside his baton. Suddenly, I heard Leela screaming with joy, 'Bhaiya!'

I could not believe my eyes! In fact, no one could believe that Satish would come at the right time. To perform the ritual where he was needed to remain present.

Quickly Bagga removed his shoes and joined in for the ceremony. Both Leela and I were ecstatic!

Without uttering a word, Satish came closer to us. Leela was crying, and I was at a loss for words or action.

Bagga was here at the right moment, participating in the marriage of his sister and best friend. All the guests were astounded and clueless about what was happening. Neverthless, looking at the happiness and emotions on our faces, they started asking questions to our parents out of curiousity.

Mataji-Pitaji and Uncle-Aunty -all were shocked but happy. Aunty and Mataji were crying and hugging each other.

As soon as the ceremony got over, Satish blessed and hugged us. He put Leela's hand in mine and said, 'I wish you both a happy married life! I am looking forward to becoming 'Mama' and a 'Chacha' (maternal and paternal Uncle) together to your children. So give me good news soon!'

Both Leela and myself were speechless, and nodded in excitement. This was a special moment for all of us.

All the guests were looking with awe, many unaware of what exactly was going on and why the police had to be called to complete the ceremony.

Satish left as quickly as he had come. He always knew the magic of disappearing into the thin air. His timely presence at our marriage conveyed his love and dedication for his family and best friend.

A strage thing happened after some time. Two more police officers entered the marriage hall. Funnily, no one paid any attention to them this time, assuming it to be another fake drama, however soon we realised that this was a serious issue, and the policemen were for real.

The first one who had entered was a British police officer. He appeared to be senior and the accompanying one was an Indian, who might be his assistant.

The British officer struck his wooden baton on the door, and shouted, 'Attention! No one will move, all stay where you are!'

He spoke in broken Hindi, 'Did anybody come here?'

I was very scared, but had to keep a brave face. I kept on thanking that Bagga had left in time fortunately.

Then Pitaji came to our rescue. He got up and came forward to reply courteously, 'No officer, there are only family members and relatives attending the marriage.'

The officer harshly announced, 'There has been a murder of a British officer, and we are in search of someone known as Gopinath Saha, Do you know him?' and looked at me, since Leela and I were seated on the dais at the ceremony spot.

I was shaking but maintaining a strong front, replied, 'No, Sir, We do not know anyone with that name.'

The officer gave me a stern look. He climbed the dais and looked around like a hawk. I was praying that no one present there would disclose what had happened a few minutes back.

Fortunately, the officer seemed satisfied and he nodded so no cross-questioning took place further.

He instructed the assistant, 'We can not locate anyone here at present. But make sure you do not leave this place till this function is over. We are also looking for the group who is helping the revolutionaries.' And then he left.

After what had happened, excitement of the event was marred.

The remaining rituals were carried out in a quiet, mechanical way. It was miraculous how Bagga was saved under these circumstances.

Once the marriage was over, we both bowed to all the elders there. My parents blessed us, and I could see a deep satisfaction in Pitaji's eyes. Leela's parents i.e my in-laws also, seemed very happy to see their daughter married to a person who did not believe in wasting his life for the freedom struggle.

Ironically, I was proud of this fact myself. I was enjoying the happiest times in my life.

After marriage, Leela accepted our house very naturally to be her own. She used to look after the needs of everyone in the family, helped my mother in the cooking and the household work. She was not demanding, though coming from a well-to-do family compared to us. Perhaps she felt more secure and familiar due to many reasons.

The happy days as people say, have a short life.

It was time to get back to work. It was mid-November when I resumed with my services at the Indian Railways.

I was greeted warmly by my colleagues, Rastogi Ji, Gupta Ji, Shankar Ji and others. I happily distributed the sweets to them. Many of them were invited for my marriage, so they started praising how good the function was.

I was surprised to learn that we had a new boss now, Kirstein Sahib. This was a big news.

What could be the reason of Guha Ji's transfer to Delhi? I was unaware about the latest developments at the office. However, as the day progressed, more facts came up.

Kirstein Sahib, a proficient Railways Offcer was called especially from London to improvise on the current accounting system at the Indian Railways. Besides, since Lucknow was a very big junction, the supervision by an expert was required. Kirsten Sahib had arrived from London for this assignment, and currently was our boss.

Soon I decided to greet Mr. Kirstein. The other employees had told me, he was already in the office at 8.30 a.m.

I knocked on his cabin door, which was replied in a kind tone, "Please come in."

I entered Kirstein Sahib's cabin. Gone was the small room with some spent wooden furniture. Instead, this was a new, larger office with latest, shining furniture and brightness all around.

I introduced myself.

"Good Morning, Sahib! I am Mukund Pandey. I have been working here, since last four months. I am resuming after my marriage."

Kirstein Sahib was pure British, who appeared to be in his mid-forties or nearing fifties. By the first impression, I was reassured that he was a nice boss to work with.

Kirstein Sahib looked at me kindly and gestured for me to take the chair opposite him.

This was a pleasant surprise for me. I do not remember sitting in front of Guha Ji in all the four months that I had served here.

"Thank you", I said nodding happily and took my seat opposite him. He shook hands with me, "Congratulations! Young man, I am happy for you. Welcome back to work!" He smiled at me. All of a sudden, I began to feel relaxed.

I tried to strike a conversation. I told him that I was on leave for my marriage, and handed over a packet of sweets prepared by Mataji.

Kirstein Sahib smiled, opened the box, picked up a laddoo and ate it. He seemed to be relishing it.

All this made me more confident to sit for a longer time in his cabin.

Marrying Leela had indeed brought a good luck for me. No wonder I had got the new boss who was so kind and humane.

Kirstein Sahib was keenly interested in knowing about the Indian customs and the rituals performed in a Hindu marriage and also about my own marriage ceremony.

He asked many questions and I was excited to share all the information with him. It was my very first attempt to communicate (in broken English added with Hindi) with any British officer after the interview.

One thing I forgot to mention is regarding my spoken English.

Yes, I could speak good English, compared to most of my friends.

Besides, it was my idiosyncrasy to imitate the British style of speaking, which actually helped me in learning the language better.

It was thrilling to talk to my British boss directly. Surprisingly, he made me comfortable by asking a few questions which was in contrast to Guha Ji.

Apparently, Kirstein Sahib was an expert in Accounts and establishing new ways of simple book keeping. This was a wonderful opportunity for me to learn a good accounting system from him.

Being an Economics student, Accounts interested me, and at times I grasped it quickly than even an experienced clerk. This was indeed a good beginning for me at the office.

The days passed by and I became a good team with Kirstein Sahib, who - I realised – appreciated my work, among all the other employees. He always praised my work and often mentioned my name as one of the best employees in Lucknow Railways.

All these facts gave a great boost to my confidence.

I gathered courage and invited Kirstein Sahib to my house for dinner, which he readily accepted.

He seemed to relish it and also was much at home. Smaller house or small means did not make him uncomfortable.

At home, everyone was in his awe, especially Pitaji for whom it was a dream like feeling to have a British guest coming for dinner.

Leela undoubtedly cooked well. Besides, I had learnt that Kirstein Sahib had problem in having food as per his choice and needs like all the British people staying in India.

I also learnt that his family was in London, and he lived here alone. As a gesture of concern and care, I often started carrying food for him at the office.

Kirstein Sahib always appreciated the different food varieties that I carried for him.

There were times when deep down in my heart, I used to remember Bagga. His dedication and purposefulness had surpassed every calculation. Sometimes I wondered if I want to stand at par with my friend in the matter of work and dedication?

Within a year, I was promoted to the post of the Accounts Manager. I had started working directly under Kirstein Sahib now. Not only that, in his absence, I was even allowed to report to the Area Chief, Campbell Sahib.

My English-speaking skills had improved, so did my dressing sense.

I was the 'Babu' of Lucknow now. I could keep my head held high with pride, while walking on the same old city roads where I grew up as a poor and weak boy.

Lalaji, hardly talked to me now, I ignored him as well.

Sometimes I got to hear the distant news of what was happening at the freedom front, but I had learnt to grow indifferent to that.

The year 1924 was coming to an end. I was living a happily married life when there was an addition to my heavenly marital life. My wife Leela was pregnant.

My happiness knew no bounds.

However, as Leela gave this good news to me, I remembered what Satish had said at the time of our marriage, his hearfelt blessings.

That day I behaved unlike my 'new' self.

I decided to go and meet Lalaji Paanwala and find out about my friend, Bagga.

He was obviously surprised to see me.

I greeted him, "Namaste! Please make a Benarasi paan for me. It has been long since I had your paan."

Lalaji smiled, and said, "Yes, Mukundji! You are now in the company of the people who smoke cigars, so you must have forgotten the paan from your motherland."

I avoided his direct stare and instead said, "Lalaji! kya haal-chaal hai Aaj-kal?" (What are the updates?)

Lalaji was surprised and looked at me intently, then spoke sarcastically, "Good you remember that other people also exist in this world. Your friend often asks me about you but he has strictly told me not to disturb you in your blissfully married life."

It was my turn to be surprised. I was thunderstruck.

Here I lived like an ostrich, oblivious of what was happening at the country's freedom struggle front, and my friend Satish, never forgot me for a moment.

It was an emotional moment for me. I asked with an excitement, "When had he been here last? I want to see him."

Lalaji answered, "He is a dedicated freedom fighter now. He is in the close committee and is sought after by the British Police. So, he would not like to meet you lest your career would be blemished. But he visits Lucknow often."

Lalaji, then shared with me some information on the whereabouts of my friend and his group.

> *He explained in short how the revolutionaries of Benaras, Agra, Allahabad, Kanpur and Lucknow were connected, which made the group very strong.*

The members of the revolutionary group often travelled to and from Lucknow on various significant occasions, and during such times, Satish used to visit Lalaji.

Banvari was imprisoned again, (which I was aware of) and it was getting difficult to get him out from the claws of the British Police.

Let me confess, I liked all the luxuries and the securities of the materialistic life on one hand, but on the other, I did miss a real friend like Satish. It was not easy to forget him with Leela in my house and meeting his parents frequently.

This time I was honest with Lalaji, 'Lalaji, when next time Satish comes to Lucknow, please tell him that I remember him, I miss him. He is going to be a Chacha and Mama (paternal and maternal Uncle) both soon.

Lalaji smiled and congratulated me, but spoke with the same sarcasm, "Congratulations! I hope your son becomes more like his uncles and inherits some of their virtues."

I happily agreed with him, then took his leave. When I reached home. Leela was waiting for me. She was looking more beautiful than ever. Perhaps she was more intuitive too.

She held a glass of water for me, and asked, "What is the news today? Anything about Bagga Bhaiya?" I did not have any answer to give her.

I excused myself and tried to avoid her by taking time to drink some water. After a few moments, I got up and evading an eye contact, just muttered, "He is well, wherever he is."

That night I waited for Bagga. I was certain that he would come and meet me, once he gets the news. I waited, but no such thing happened that night or for the next few days.

After about five days, when I was fast asleep, early in the morning, there was a soft tapping on the window of my room, overlooking at the backside of the house. I woke up with a start and opened it.

I asked, "Who is there?"

Slowly a shadow emerged from the darkness and handed over a chit to me and before I could grasp what was happening, vanished from the window.

I opened it with shaking hands, which just read, 'Amavasya, 12 at Bada Imambara.'

Amavasya is a no moon night. Naturally, this day would be the safest day hence, my friend chose it, so that I could go and meet him.

However, I was not happy with Satish. Why would he not come to meet me at home? Has he killed someone? Or is he involved in some dangerous activity? I must know about this.

Lost in these thoughts, I slept off again.

The first thing I did in the morning was to find out when was the Amavasya day. It was on the 8th December.

Today was the 5th December,1924. Yes, three more days to go.

I had decided that I will locate a safe place in the Bara Imambara and meet Satish there.

Bada Imambara was a famous hitorical place with a maze called the 'Bhulbhulaiya' also known as the Asfi Mosque. The Imambara complex was built by Asaf-ud-Daula, the Nawab of Awadh in 1784.

Only the people who knew a way out of the maze, could dare to enter the place. Naturally, Since Satish and I had grown up in Lucknow, it was an easy game for both of us to meet there without getting lost.

Nonetheless, due to these reasons, it was important to confirm the exact meeting place.

Hence after office hours, I went to meet Lalaji at his paan shop.

As Lalaji saw me approaching, he gave a knowing smile. Thankfully he did not appear to be sarcastic or complaining with me.

This was very encouraging. "Lalaji Namaste!"

He replied, "Aao beta! Kaise ho?" (Welcome! How are you?)

I replied, "I am fine, Lalaji. But I am looking for some shelter. I don't know where can I find it?"

Lalaji was sharp as ever, and updated with the latest information. 'If you feel lost, why don't you go at the back under that big banyan tree, since you need protection?"

Despite of the fact that I did not belong to Satish's group, ironically I was gradually learning their ways of communication.

I knew that I need not say anything further with him and left.

Next three days were the longest ever days of waiting span of my life. I could not focus on my office work. My mind was completely occupied with the thoughts of meeting Bagga, and questioning myself, if I was doing the right thing by putting my faithfulness towards the British Government at stake.

During the office hours, whenever I talked to Kirstein Sahib, I felt guilty like a thief who has stolen something precious.

Leelavati Narrates

I was not supposed to be alive, but I survived. Perhaps, my sisters and I were not supposed to live being born as girls. Our parents had five children, two sons and three daughters.

I was the last one to be born after my two brothers- Banvari Bhaiya and Satish Bhaiya and next two sisters - Suryakumari Didi and Jaswanti Didi. When Jaswanti Didi was born, our grandmother declared that it was good to have so many children but two daughters were more than enough for the family.

However, luckily or by chance, I was saved from sure death by the doctors at the time of my birth, and accepted hesitatingly, by my parents.

As my grandmother learnt about my birth, she kept on taunting my mother, why she wanted a third daughter, which was like one more burden on the family.

My mother must have been badly nagged by her for a long time and would not have known what to do with me.

All this I learnt much later from my mother.

She had finally found a terrifying solution - she started giving me opium in small doses during the day. Ironically, this was a usual method adopted by many parents having a girl child in the village. My mother was advised by an old aunt to use opium since it was a safe method, till the final decision was taken.

Eventually, as an infant I would sleep all day unstirred. This threw me completely out from the household scene. Consequently, my grandmother even forgot to notice my presence in the house.

Much to my good luck, many Government officers lived in the houses around us in our area, and a police constable's family lived in our neighbourhood. The wife of the constable, Sarita Devi was friendly with Mataji and used to come to our house very often.

Looking at my condition, she used to ask many questions to Mataji. It was evident that there was something abnormal about a three-month-old child, lying lifelessly for the whole day without crying or demanding for milk.

One day she called a government authorised doctor for Police department, especially for me.

When the Doctor checked me, he was shocked to see my condition and in strict words, told my grandmother and mother not to dope me, or he would complain and get them jailed.

His warning scared the elders of our family, and from that day onwards, I was stopped giving opium. I was looked after like the other children of the family. Thus, I survived.

After this incident, Sarita Devi made sure that I was brought up in a healthy environment and given proper food, and nourishment.

She often used to bring milk and biscuits for me and my siblings. But she always exhibited a special favour towards me.

This continued for almost eight years, till the police constable's family came to live in our neighbourhood.

As I started growing up abiding by the universal rule of the 'Survival of the fittest', my survival instincts made me stronger than the other girls of my age.

All the children grew up healthily in our family as a result and also started going to nearby municipal school at Sarita Devi's recommendation. My father often thanked the British Government for these values, the importance of which I learnt many years later.

However, it was then that the Constable Saheb was transferred to Calcutta, since Calcutta was being turned into an inferno by the freedom fighters, and needed a stronger and bigger Police force there to curb them, as Saritadevi told my mother.

Once again, our family's orthodox values surfaced. Besides, my father could not afford all his children to be sent to school, so the family decided that the daughters – Suryakumari Didi, Jaswanti Didi and I should stop going to school now onwards, instead help mother in the household, cooking and other chores.

Among all brothers and sisters, my favourite was Satish Bhaiya, whom everyone called 'Bagga', and I was his favourite sister. He fondly called me 'Muniya' and would always get goodies, to share with me first, and then with the others.

Though my education did not continue further than the 5th Standard, Bagga Bhaiya taught me the basic skills of life to become strong and confident, when I was growing up.

In some time, Surya Kumari Didi and Jaswanti Didi who were seven and five years elder to me, were engaged to the boys much older to them, and were both married off at Allahabad and Kanpur respectively, when was hardly seven years of age.

Since my grandfather was highly respected in our caste, the marriage had to be somewhat opulent and we had to provide good gifts to my sisters and their in-laws. In spite of a high social status, we were not rich. Pitaji worked as a clerk, and it was not easy for him to spend money lavishly for the two marriages. As a result,he incurred some debt.

Pitaji and grandmother were very keen that I should also be married off along with my sisters and had already started seeking marriage proposals for me, to avoid the added expenses for my marriage, but Satish Bhaiya and Mataji opposed. Bhaiya disagreed openly, whereas mother showed silent protest.

Ironically, my sisters did not live long to enjoy a happy married life.

Jaswanti Didi died during her first delivery after one and a half years of marriage. She could not cope up with the laborious work at her in- laws' house.

Her husband was a farmer. She had to do all the household work since early morning and then join her husband later during the day at their farm.

She had an old grandmother-in-law who used to live with them, and would speak bitter words to my sister all the time.

When Jaswanti Didi was pregnant, she did not get proper medical care, and suffered with severe aneamia. We requested them to bring her to Lucknow, but her husband and grandmother-in-law refused.

Eventually, her delivery procedure was carried out at home without any medical help. It was very shocking that after giving birth to a baby boy she died of internal bleeding.

We lost Jaswanti Didi due to sheer negligence on part of her husband and in-laws. But this was no loss to them and they remained unaffected. My brother-in-law was married off within two months of my sister Jaswanti Didi's death.

We brought her infant son to our house. He was named Birendra.

Hardly six months must have passed to the sad demise of Jaswanti Didi, when we received the news of Surya Kumari Didi's illness.

As soon as we received this news, Pitaji and Banvari Bhaiya rushed to visit her. But by the time they reached her house, they were told that she had already passed away. No reason or explanation was provided. Surya Kumari Didi's in-laws had already cremated her by then, without informing us.

This terrible treatment to my sisters was shocking and unbelievable, although we could not do anything afterwards.

Surya Kumari Didi was happily married, or so we always thought. Though people used to come up with the stories of her in-laws being relentless and merciless towards her, she had never complained of any trouble from anyone from her in-laws' side.

Hardly a month before her illness, Surya Kumari Didi had visited us, when Mataji had gifted her two new sarees, and some ornaments for the approaching Diwali festival in the next month.

Mataji was shattered as she was very attached to my sisters, especially Surya Kumari Didi, and her death always remained a mystery to us.

It was difficult to bear the loss of both my sisters. It took a long time for all of us to get over these shocks, and secretly my parents were thankful that I was not married off in a hurry.

Everyone was unhappy in the house for a long time, and my grandmother passed away within a year crying after her two grand daughters.

After losing my sisters so suddenly, I removed the word ‘marriage’ from my dictionary.

Even my parents and brothers hesitated in getting me married in haste into an unknown family, though they were also worried about finding a suitable match for me, as I was growing older, and was almost in my late teens.

The society which believed in the child marriages could not bear the girls remaining unmarried for long, even if they had to give away their lives like my sisters.

Satish Bhaiya was firm that he would find a good match for me. He had a friend (rather best friend) named Mukund Pandey, who was two years elder to him, almost the age of Banvari Bhaiya.

One day, when the winter was getting over and the spring was setting in, Mukund Ji came running to our house with Birendra (Biru). In fact, Satish Bhaiya had called him urgently, Biru told me later. At that time, I was in the kitchen with Mataji.

Bagga Bhaiya, Banvari Bhaiya and Mukund Ji, all three had been talking in the backyard of our house for a long time. I could only hear some heated arguments between Bagga Bhaiya and Mukund Ji.

Biru was listening to the discussion hiding behind the doors. After a while he came and told me that it was about the freedom movement.

I had come to know about it from Banvari Bhaiya. He always used to talk about the freedom movement and that some powerful leaders were trying to throw away Gora log from our country with the help of this movement.

There was a leader whom everyone respected and followed, Gandhi was his name. He had decided not to cooperate with the British Raj.

Biru said, 'Mausi (maternal aunt) Please prepare some tea for them.'

So I prepared tea and took it in the backyard, where they were sitting. The backyard was my favourite place in the whole big house.

Yes, our house was big, and looking after it took a lot of time and effort. I had seen mother taking care of everything in the house, all the time. I had started helping her more often for the household work, once I realised how difficult it was.

After the morning chores or often during the day, I used to sit in the backyard, where Dadaji (grand father) had planted so many trees. There were many flowering plants like the sunflower, mogra, roses and many bigger trees. Spring used to bring beautiful colours to them, and whole of the backyard looked like a small garden.

I used to talk with these trees, and they talked back to me, though everyone in the house found it to be crazy.

That day, when I entered the backyard, I could see that Bagga Bhaiya was very disturbed.

Mukund Ji also seemed disturbed. He kept talking about the college and examinations.

I did not want to be part of their discussion, so I went in the house after serving tea to them.

The discussion seemed to have ended soon and I saw Mukundji leaving after some time.

Within a few minutes, Banvari Bhaiya too went away.

Then Bagga Bhaiya called me again in the backyard. "Muniya, did you hear anything discussed here? Do you know what has happened?"

I shook my head to say "No".

Bagga Bhaiya held my hand and made me sit next to him. "I am sharing this with you since you are my dear sister. The mission I was planning to join soon, the Non-Cooperation Movement, has been called off."

I was listening intently, trying to understand what he said.

He continued, "But my mission was not the Non-Cooperation Movement, Muniya. No one understands that."

"I want to free my country, my motherland, and I am determined to do anything for the freedom."

I recalled now. Since childhood, Bagga Bhaiya used to tell me, "Muniya, If I get involved into the freedom struggle, you will help me, won't you?"

I used to agree happily. The freedom fight was always like a fairy tale to me.

"Muniya, my life is not going to be the same anymore. Perhaps, I may not study further. I have to carry out some responsibilities. But promise me that you will look after yourself and Mataji & Pitaji."

Before he could say anything further, Mataji called me in the kitchen, so our talk ended abruptly.

After a few days, Bagga Bhaiya found opportunity to talk with me again, when both of us were sitting alone in the backyard.

"I want to ask you something, Muniya. As you know, Mukund is my close friend. Though we both are very different in our principles and priorities, he is a wise boy. You are my dear sister, and I want you to marry someone who will keep you happy. You will not find a better husband than Mukund. He will never join the freedom struggle. Instead, he wants to settle well in life and become a Government officer. Whoever marries him will be very happy and lucky too."

I did not know what to say. I got up and began walking towards the kitchen.

I stopped when I heard Bagga Bhaiya calling me from behind, "Leela, I may not be able to see you any more. That is why I said all this to you"

I was shocked, and could hardly speak, "Why are you saying this, Bhaiya?"

'Muniya, A lot has to be done for the country. We are already lagging behind badly in the fight against the King. They are much advanced in technology. Besides, we do not have support from our own leaders."

Gradually the situation dawned upon me. "You are going away Bhaiya? Where will you go? Where will you stay?"

"Muniya, People who want to achieve their goals can not afford to sit at home and wait for the right opportunity. We have to take risks and create opportunities for ourselves."

Bagga Bhaiya's words meant the world to me. Now I also realised why he was talking about my marriage.

After losing both my sisters, I had never thought about my marriage.

All the elderly relatives, especially women, used to taunt and mock me that no one would marry me now. However, it did not matter to me anymore. After seeing my sisters die pathetically, it was a safer and wiser choice to remain unmarried.

This suggestion from Bagga Bhaiya came as a surprise. How much he thought of my future happiness!

> *Of course, Mukund Ji was not the best candidate for marriage. Nothing romantic could be connected with him. Neither he nor I had seen each other from this viewpoint.*

He was a thin, dark-complexioned boy, unlike my brothers. He had plain features and was very shy. In the situations where my brothers used to take a lead, he would sit quietly behind and discuss what was right and what was wrong. He was more of a studious type of person.

He never fought with anyone. I had always seen him worrying about his mother's health. He obediently followed his father's orders. On the other hand, one could not deny that he was someone who could provide security and respect to his family.

It was obvious that Satish Bhaiya must have thought about all these things.

I had to give my reply now. I could neither postpone the decision, nor could feel the excitement while deciding about my marriage.

However, one thing was certain, that my brother would select the best match for me.

It was more due to this reason than any liking for Mukund Ji that I answered in affirmative.

"Bhaiya, if you think he is the right person, I will marry him."

Bagga Bhaiya seemed relieved by my answer. "I knew you will agree. After losing our two dear sisters,

I want to make certain that you are happily and safely married. Mukund and his parents will welcome you in their house."

Bhaiya was probably right in saying this.

We were Baniyas by caste and the zamindaars. Mukund Ji was a Brahmin with a modest background.

Their family came from the background of the pujari (Hindu Priest) community, one who performs religious rituals for people. His grandfather was a Pundit, and collected Prasadi (offerings) as a means for livelihood.

Both our families knew each other well. Mukund Ji's mother - Usha Devi was very kind to me whenever I went to their house. She always gave me something to eat from the Prasadi.

Mukund Ji's father, though known to be strict about his principles, liked both my brothers and me.

Bagga Bhaiya looked happy too.

"Muniya, I will convey this to Mataji. Since I might not be around for your wedding. I wish you good luck in life."

He came near me and put his hand on my head to bless me.

I could not say anything. He had fulfilled his promise to our parents to find a good match for me. I started crying, but Bagga Bhaiya did not wait to pacify me. I knew that he got very emotional.

I hardly talked to Bagga Bhaiya, for the next two days after this, but my mind ran over the conversation with him at least a hundred times, and each time my decision to marry Mukund Ji appeared more and more positive.

I also realised that it was important to be strong and practical in life.

Then something terribly shocking and unexpected happened. Banvari Bhaiya was jailed. We were all shaken up, especially Mataji and Pitaji.

Bagga Bhaiya frequently visited Banavri Bhaiya in the jail. He told everyone at home, that he would have to run about a lot for his release.

Banvari Bhaiya's case was taken up to the local court.

Since the offence for which he was jailed was a simple one, everyone at home was expecting that he would be released soon, and that the things would be normal as before.

Unfortunately, the turn of events changed lives of all the family members completely -. as if a storm had struck us all!

Bagga Bhaiya was secretly trying to contact the group of freedom fighters which he was planning to join.

In the meanwhile, he talked to Mukundji's parents about my marriage with Mukund Ji.

This was a very happy news for my parents, who had lost all hopes of my marriage. This brought a new life to them, and their smiling faces made us forget about the other difficulties of life, one being Banvari Bhaiya in the jail.

Mataji was a very practical woman. She told Pitaji that Mukund Ji was an eligible boy for me to get married to, and we should not waste any time now, and to fix a meeting with his family. He also agreed with her saying that Mukund Ji will prosper in life one day with his hard work and sincerity.

Thus, my Parents planned to meet Mukund Ji's Parents on the coming Sunday.

It was lamentable that Bagga Bhaiya left the house without informing anyone before the meeting could take place regarding my marriage.

Though I was certain that Mukund Ji knew about Bagga Bhaiya's decision to leave home, no one else in our family knew anything about it.

This disturbed and delayed the meeting, as the mediator had disappeared. Consequently, we had to wait till Mukund Ji's college exams got over.

In the meanwhile, Mukund Ji used to come to our house and felt responsible for us now that Bagga Bhaiya and Banvari Bhaiya both were not there.

Sometimes difficult circumstances happen for a reason. Due to such unforeseen happenings, communication was live between our families, and also between Mukund Ji and me.

But my parents wanted a formal confirmation about our engagement.

Finally, as the day was decided, my parents went to meet Mukund Ji's parents in the evening. It appeared that they had sensed it already, and it was just a matter of formal confirmation to tie a marital knot between Mukund Ji and me.

Uncle and Aunty greeted us with warmth. They had no reason to deny the proposal. In fact, their son had done them proud by becoming a good citizen of the British India. As a bonus, he was also marrying a zamindar's grand-daughter.

Once their approval was received, both parents congratulated one another.

After returning home, mother narrated to me everything in details, and I kept on asking her umpteen questions, to which she happily replied.

This was a very happy occasion in our house after a long time. My parents were more delighted by the fact that the whole process was so simplified, and looked much ahead of time. There was no pressure of any sort from Mukund Ji's parents.

An official announcement was made about my engagement with Mukund Ji, in a simple way. Our family was still passing through the trauma of Banvari Bhaiya and Bagga Bhaiya's life events.

However, we often invited Mukund Ji and his parents for meals, and as per our custom, gave them gifts, which was in fact more of a reflection of my parents' happiness.

In a short span of time, Mukund Ji and his parents accepted me with affection in their family.

Since I was their would-be daughter-in- law, Aunty used to call me frequently to their house to teach me knick knacks and to talk about her family.

Mukund Ji wanted to wait for our marriage till he got a proper job. Few months passed, and my parents started to panic, doubting if this marriage would work out for me or not.

However, after some wait Mukund Ji's job at the IndianRailways got confirmed, and they had no reason to delay our marriage.

Everything was going on smoothly now, with the marriage date fixed in the month of October.

A week prior to our marriage, mother took me to buy a saree at a saree shop, from where I selected a specialBenarasi saree.

I was going through a collection of sarees from the shop, and I kept on finding something amiss in each of them. No saree was a perfect combination of red and green colour, with the right silk texture.

Suddenly, I saw a shadow emerging from the dark corner of the shop just after afew moments.

I was busy looking at the sarees and did not realise it immediately. After a few moments I heard someone calling me "Muniya!" .

I was surprised, and got up to see who was calling me by my nick-name.

Then I found a human figure hiding in a corner. This was scary! I slowly went towards that corner.

That person had covered his face completely. Before I could scream, surprisingly he handed over a packet to me and whispered softly, "Muniya, Best wishes and blessings for your marriage."

It took me some time to come to my senses and look searchingly in that direction, but there was no one to be found now. For a moment, I wondered, if this was a dream or just an imagination? Alas! here was a packet in my hands.

I returned to where Mataji was sitting and with teary-eyes told her, 'Ma, I have received my first wedding gift. And who else could give this gift to me but Bagga Bhaiya.'

Ma was shocked, and became pale with grief. We opened the packet, there was a very colourful red and green Benarasi saree in it. It was exactly the type of saree I was looking for!

Both Ma and I started crying. I touched the saree to my forehead in a gesture of respect and said, "Bagga Bhaiya! I wish you could have waited."

Mataji was very upset. We left the shop immediately and rushed towards home. The shopping of my saree was taken care of.

"How did he manage to buy this saree? Bagga Bhaiya exactly knows my taste and favourite colours."

There were so many questions on my mind, and Mataji's anxiety to have missed meeting her son, but there was no one to answer them.

This incident left a deep impact on my mind. Both Mataji and I remembered and talked about Bagga Bhaiya for a long time. As it is said, time is the healer. In due course, though this incident and the meeting with Bhaiya was not forgotten, but rested in our hearts silently and the preparations for marriage continued in full swing.

> *Thankfully, Mukund Ji was granted a long leave from his office, which was very exciting and helpful in making various arrangements, and ease out running around when the guests would arrive.*

Mukundji looked very happy, and everyone remarked that my face was gleaming as well.

His mother kept saying that "My son is very lucky to have such a nice wife."

The days flew by very quickly in happiness and anticipation of celebrations and the day of marriage arrived.

No day is happier for any girl than the day of her marriage and I was already in my dream world oblivious of everything around me.

Since morning the hustle-bustle was on. The rituals and functions were going on in full excitement, and all our relatives were there to share in our happiness.

Pitaji had made sure that the decorations and the preparations were done in style. Special helpers were assigned the task of making the whole place colourful and bright with a lot of flowers and lights.

Pitaji knew that I was very fond of flowers and he wanted to show his love and happiness by making our marriage a memorable one.

The food was made and arranged in ample quantities for all the guests. In spite of our limited resources, marriage was celebrated with lot of splendour and enjoyment.

Of course, at every step, both the brothers – Banvari Bhaiya and Satish Bhaiya were missed, but we had to keep the painful thoughts aside and enjoy whatever life had offered to us.

Mukund Ji's family did not expect or ask for any dowry or special gifts from us, which was highly appreciated by everyone. My parents were happy to see that I had found a good husband though I had to wait long for marriage.

They had already lost the other two daughters in a tragicway, and were very sceptical about me.

The marriage ceremony began at around 10.30 a.m as per the auspicious time. We took our vows and performed the sacred wedding rituals round the pious fire amidst chanting of the mantras by Pundits.

I was very nervous, since I knew that for the next ritual, presence of the bride's brothers was essential.

Pujari (Hindu Priest) announced, "Now the bride's brother will perform the puja (ritual)."

There was complete silence in the marriage hall. Everyone looked at each other.

It was really unfortunate that none of my two brothers were there to complete my marriage ceremony.

In fact, the Jail Suprintendent had agreed to grant bail to Banvari Bhaiya to attend the marriage but sadly Bhaiya had not reached the marriage place as yet.

Suddenly we saw a policeman entering the marriage hall in a hurry, with a baton in his hand and a big, curved moustache on his face.

He was coming straight towards the dais where the ceremony was going on.

All of us were scared. Why was a policeman coming towards the wedding venue? This was the last thing we wanted at this moment. Mukund Ji muttered nervously, "Police seems to have found out my connection with Satish."

The policeman came straight to us, where the ceremony was going on where we were seated along with the Priest. He put aside his baton.

When I looked at him, I was ecstatic to see that he was none other than Bagga Bhaiya.

I exclaimed, "Bhaiya!"

Bagga Bhaiya, the magician was here at the right time.

Then he removed his shoes and joined us for the ceremony. Everyone in the family was jubilant. I could not stop my tears.

He peacefully performed all the rituals necessary by bride's brother.

This was the most memorable moment. My happiness knew no bounds. Mukund Ji, Pitaji and Mataji- all of them were thrilled to see Bagga Bhaiya at the right time of the marriage.

When everything was completed as desired, Bagga Bhaiya touched Pitaji and Mataji's feet, hugged me and Mukund Ji and asked permission to leave. We were too happy to stop him from going away.

In less than ten minutes of Bagga Bhaiya leaving, two police officers entered the marriage hall. They were of course the real British Police officials.

I was certain that nothing could go wrong now, when I had two strong brothers who had challenged the British Government.

After some shouting and a futile search, one of them left the venue.

Once the senior British officer left,
the policeman who was Indian was
not to be worried about.

Thus my marriage to Mukund Ji was celebrated in perfect manner with rituals, and I was thankful to God for everything, especially for such a dramatic presence of Bagga Bhaiya.

I considered myself fortunate, to have married in a family where I would be looked after with love and care. Naturally, it did not take me long to settle down in the new life- married life with Mukund Ji and the days flew in happiness

Their house was much smaller compared to where I had lived all these years.

But Mukund Ji, Mataji and Pitaji were very kind to me, so I started enjoying my life fully.

Soon it was time for my husband to resume his job.

This was a proud matter for all of us that he worked for the Indian Railways.

Then the most wonderful thing happened. I was going to have a baby.

This news spread happiness in Mukund Ji's family and more so to my parents.

Perhaps, for my parents this was a good way to get over the pain of the absence of their sons.

❑

The Prestigious Indian Railways Project

Kirstein Narrates

It was the last week of February 1923, and I was enjoying the vacation with my family in Scotland.

I had combined my leave with a weekend. It was not easy amidst a busy office routine.

Finally, with my wife Martha and our two children Joshua and Jane, aged 7 and 5, we had just reached Scotland by train. We checked into my favourite hotel, one of the most picturesque places that I had booked which had a beautiful lakeside cottage.

The late winters, with a pleasant weather, made the surroundings very lively and enjoyable, as we had been looking forward to.

Martha and the children had made various plans of sight seeing, fishing, boating, etc. I was sitting with a glass of beer at the poolside in the company of my favourite book by Shakespeare.

In no time we settled ourselves in this beautiful place.

Next day, as I wished "Good morning" to the Hotel Manager at the reception, he quipped, "Sir, there is a telegram for you."

Slightly taken aback, I took it and opened it, which read, "This is regarding your transfer order by the Head Office. Return soon."

Receiving a transfer order was not unusual for me. In my Railways job this was more of a rule than an exception.

Frankly speaking, I did not appreciate timing of the transfer order. This was the last thing I could have asked for.

Besides, reason for the urgency of my transfer was beyond my understanding.

With a heavy heart and many promises to my family for more exciting vacations, when the next opportunity came my way, we returned to London by the evening train.

On our way back, both Martha and I kept guessing which city or town we would be transferred to this time.

Martha was very optimistic, "George, my gut feeling says that we will be transferred to Manchester. Aunt Agatha has a huge property there. How I have always longed to stay in her villa!"

Incidentally, I disapproved of Martha's Aunt Agatha completely.

However, looking at the situation now, if we had to stay in Manchester, I could not be unhappy with her for many reasons.

However, Aunt Agatha's presence in an unknown city would be a relief to my family as we had not many friends or other relatives there and the issue of children's schooling could be sorted out through her influencial connections.

Though, I was not sure and did not really know what my transfer destination would be. I said to her, "Dear, there are many other transfer places possible. The Railway Department is coming up with many new routes. I am afraid Manchester might not be the place we will be sent to." But it was difficult to convince Martha till I actually received the transfer order.

In the meanwhile, as we reached home, Martha did not waste a minute, and we were at her parents' house the next evening to break the news.

On the dinner table, Martha's father wished me, "George, congratulations on your transfer to Manchester. It is a beautiful city. We have spent our days of youth in this glamorous city. I can also recommend your name for the 'Club Rodrigues' which allows only the elite. Though, I would suggest that you carry my recommendation letter.

I thanked him and nodded. 'Daddy! That would be so wonderful! Nonetheless, I would request you to wait till I get a formal transfer letter from the office tomorrow."

Martha's mother looked at her daughter proudly.

"Let me tell you this, Martha, Aunt Agatha may boast of a beautiful villa with a well spread garden of a few acres, but the furniture that she owns can never match with what your grandfather had collected."

Martha's father affirmed this.

Before the furniture of Aunt Agatha's home would be further criticised, I announced that it was time to retire, as I had to report early at the office tomorrow.

As my luck would have it, morning saw me in the cabin of my boss, Mr. Tumbleton. He seemed excited to see me.

I assumed it to be a good sign, which was a grave mistake.

He shook hands warmly and gestured me to sit. "Welcome George! I am sure you must have received the wire that was sent to you. At the same time, I am extremely sorry to disturb your family vacation."

I protested humbly, "Not at all Sir. I respect my work more than anything else."

Mr. Tumbleton smiled. My experience with him as a boss warned me, that this was not a good sign.

I waited for the unexpected to follow. "Dear George, let me tell you that you have proved as one of the best team members at the Railways Office here, and your work is highly appreciated at the head office. Congratulations!"

He paused, and I could not prevent from feeling proud of myself. I could only mutter, "Thank you, Sir!"

He continued, "Do you remember that I had discussed the 'Acworth Committee' report with you last time? The project we have undertaken at one of the colonised country, India. It has now gained the status of being one of the most prestigious projects, next to the American Railways Project after the War."

He added enthusiastically, "As suggested by the 'Famine Commissioners' many years ago, thousands of kilometres of railway network is being set up there. The first level of project is almost complete."

"Not only that, it is considered to be one of the biggest revenue generating systems for that country. As a result, His Excellency Mr. Acworth has suggested to have a separate accounting system for the Railways. You can guess what a mammoth task it is! To carry out the implementation of these changes, we have formed a committee here."

"The first committee that was formed consisted of....", he stopped midway and said casually, "Well, all the details are in this report here." He handed me a bulky file. I got up to receive it.

I was all ears to learn about my transfer.

"In fact, I have been fortunate to have been selected as a committee member. I was to look after this project and was to be sent to India. However, unforseen circumstances have prevented me from going to India."

He concluded, "My wife, Susan is not keeping good health after our third child, Wilbert's birth. She has turned very anaemic and needs personal care and attention. As a result, it has been unanimously decided that you will go to India, you are capable of shouldering this responsibility well, George. Your expertise will be very useful for the 'Acworth plan' completion. I am confident that you will not allow my absence to be felt for this project."

So this was it.

I was searching for words to say something, but was too dumbstruck by this news, that came almost as a blow.

Was Mr. Tumbleton really excited, or was he relieved?

"Of course, we have an experts team already working on this project since some time at the Head office in India, at Delhi, in assistance with some local experts."

"You will be accompanied by other team members from London, and here is the list of places each one is posted at. You have to work initially at Delhi, and later at Lucknow, which is the centre of one of the biggest states under the British rule, the United Provinces. I assure you that you will enjoy your stay there."

It took me a few seconds to react to this decision. "Thank you Sir, I am privileged."

I had joined the British Railways immediately after my graduation from the prestigious London University, when I was barely 20 years of age, and had been serving the company for almost 25 years now. I was proud of this fact, and my career had seen a rising graph of promotions all throughout.

Perhaps I should take pride in being selected for this mission I told myself.

"We will make certain that your wife and children follow you in next six months' time, or a little more. By then you will be well settled and accustomed to the systems there. Wherever you go in India, a good accommodation will be provided to you, and the arrangements will be made for the education of your children at a Missionary school." So everything was already taken care of and finalised.

"This is the Agenda of the Acworth's report for you to have a look in the meanwhile, so that you can prepare accordingly."

Obviously, this was an order and not an option.

Thanking Mr. Tumbleton, I went to my working table, and sat down as if dazed.

I could sense my collegues' eyes following me, looking at my demeanour.

As I glanced through the report, it began as follows:

[1920; An East Indian Railway Committee is being constituted under the Chairmanship of Sir William Acworth. This committee consists of 10 members and among them 3 are Indians viz. V S Sriniwas Sastri (Member of Council of States), Purshottam Das Thakurdas (representing Indian Commercial Interests) and Rajendra Nath Mukherjee.

The Acworth Committee recommends the consolidation and nationalisation of the Indian Railways.

Based upon the recommendations of Acworth Committee, the Finances of the Railways are advised to be separated at the earliest and the Railway Budget should be separated from the General Budget.

Key Recommendations

The Acworth Committee recommendations are to be passed by September, 1924 as the Separation Convention. Separation of the railway finances from general finances will be by far the most important reform in financial management.]

There was a lot more information, and all this was ready for me to read and prepare for India's project.

I read the report thoroughly and realised that an enormous task awaited me in the distant subcontinent.

Obviously, I was expected to be on duty at my earliest. The earliest would be at least two to three months, by the time I reached the destination via sea travel.

My wife's dream about Manchester and Aunt Agatha will have to wait for some more years.

Instead of Aunt Agatha and her royal treatment, here I was to sail by the ship 'Augusta' to India on the next Sunday morning.

What followed the transfer order remained to be imagined.

The news of the change in my transfer destination took even lesser time to reach Martha's parents and our shopping plans for the fancy clothes for Manchester trip were replaced by necessary medicines and vaccinations.

Martha's mother had no further interest left in discussing my job transfer. Perhaps I was lowered by a grade or two in my in-laws' eyes.

Albeit according to me and my collegues, this was certainly a prestigious career opportunity for me.

Martha being the only daughter of her rich parents, there were questions raised if she should follow me to India, a country where no comfort of any kind could be guranteed, a country of unknown languages, a scary place with animals roaming on the roads.

Thankfully, unlike her parents, Martha had an adventure streak in her. This might be one of the reasons that she decided to join me in India with the children, whenever it was possible.

In fact, all the discussion and criticism about India by my esteemed in- laws had resulted in curiosity. Hence, we looked forward to visiting this mystical country.

There were many stories and myths about Hindustan, which we had heard from the kith and kin of the officers and their families, who were posted there.

At the subconscious level, I realised that I was destined to visit India someday and that time had now arrived.

With positive thoughts, we started packing for the unknown world.

One of our neighbours, Mr. Johnson's brother was a Chief of Army at Delhi, in India.

I decided to meet Mr. Johnson. He was very helpful in preparing my mind for staying in India.

Mr. Johnson was a retired Civil engineer, and a person with a pleasant disposition.

I paid him a visit at his beautiful villa, after office hours on Friday and he invited me to join him for coffee.

"So how do you feel about being posted to Hindustan, Mr. Kirstein?"

He asked this million-pound question, while handing me a cup of aromatic coffee.

In his large drawing room, I half got up from the sofa and taking the cup in my hands, replied, 'Thank you, Mr. Johnson. Though I feel to some extent that I am deported.

"I can not also deny that excitement to visit India is growing in me."

Mr. Johnson nodded, "My dear friend, isn't it unbelievable, when one thinks that in the eight large provinces there are but a thousand British civilians to carry out orders of the Government? Altogether members of the ruling race is only about ten to a million of the people they govern. One is tempted to ask by what magic are these millions held in check? Is it the fear of the armed British forces ready to enforce the law that gives a weight to each command?"

This thought had never occurred to me before. But yes, there must be something magical about the way the British had prevailed there overtaking many of our neighbours.

For that matter, the British were proudly ruling over many other countries in the world for almost half a century now.

"I agree with you, Mr. Johnson. In fact, don't you feel that at any moment, the residents of this country can start a revolt and take the administration in their hands? Something similar to what happened some fifty years ago?"

Mr. Johnson put his coffee cup down to pour some more coffee into it. "Exactly, Mr. Kirstein."

He carried on, "I will give you an example. An old man once walking on a property in Scotland, was asked by a stranger if the estate was his. 'No,' He answered, 'but the view is mine.' The reply may be taken as an illustration of the enthusiasm with which an Englishman regards his work in India."

"It is not as a person, but as a patriot that he is proud of its importance."

Mr. Johnson's words were so inspiring that I began preparing myself mentally for the long journey. It was the perspective that mattered i.e., to be good in your work as an Englishman, wherever you may be.

He gave me the address of his brother in Delhi, and mentioned that he will write to him as well about my posting in India.

His knowledge about India was limited only to the letters he received from his brother. As a result, he could not provide much information to me.

To sum it up, he said, "So my dear friend, I wish you all the very best in your mission. It will be more of an adventure where there is no civilised way of living, and as a paradox, you may at times also feel at the top of the world, considering the respect and attention that you get there."

Ironically, the image that he created of India affirmed my belief that it was my destiny which was taking me to India.

Within a week I saw myself boarding the ship that was going to take me to Bombay (today's Mumbai). Reaching Bombay, it was going to be minimum three months long journey, considering that everything went off well.

Martha and children had come to see me off at the port, which was a very emotional moment for all of us.

How I wish they could accompany me all the way to India.

Fortunately, we had a good domestic help, a full time maid staying with our family since Joshua — our first child was born, and I was assured that Martha will not have too much trouble to cope up with household work in my absence.

Besides, her parents and brother lived not far off from where we stayed.

I had lost my father, and my mother lived with my elder brother in Scotland. In case of need, they were always there.

However, the uncertainty of when Martha and children will be able to join me in India loomed over our minds.

Two days prior to our departure, I was given a farewell by the Office Management, along with four other officers who were to take up this assignment or a similar one in the various cities in India.

India being vast in dimensions, there was no certainty about meeting each other, once we reached there.

With a heavy heart, and bagful of mixed feelings, which included excitement, adventure, and fear of the unknowns among many other apprehensions, I left the shores of London to sail to India.

It appeared to be a good beginning, with the passengers on board looking very familiar so that I did not feel uncomfortable at all. It was more like a get-together of fine British Officers in majority, who were deputed with various tasks in different departments, most of them going to India. There were some Senior Officers who were returning to work, and were fortunate to travel with their families.

However, the majority of us were single, and it was an emotional sight watching them bidding farewell to their families.

Of course, there was a battalion of soldiers on the ship. Most of them were of Indian origin, who had fought for the war here, and were returning to their home country.

They were put up on the lower deck, and thankfully we were going to see them only when we reach the shores of Hindustan.

An outspoken officer remarked, "One really wonders whether sacrificing personal lives of hundreds of accomplished British is worth for ruling over the countries at the other end of the world?" but everyone turned deaf to his remark.

I had always hoped it to be America whenever I got an opportunity to travel abroad, since several railway projects were being carried out there by our company.

Though, I had no reason to complain about my sea travel, with good food, good company and nothing much to do, except reading books which I had carried with me. Thus this travel was a fascinating experience for me, since I was stepping out of the United Kingdom for the first time in my life. At times, it was also natural to forget the purpose of my travel during the three months' journey.

As the journey began, amidst the vast Atlantic Sea, we all started talking to each other, introducing ourselves.

It was surprising as well as relieving to some extent when a few of them praised their life in India.

"Heard that there are elephants and snakes on the road." Mr. Patrick seemed petrified.

One enthusiastic officer butted in.

"No, no, my dear fellow! There is no such thing! Of course, you do not get to live very comfortably, with a limited number of trains and tongas for commuting, or lack of a very clean environment, but let me tell you, their readiness to provide services is I would say, comes very handy. And do not forget, we are ruling over them."

"The food is very cheap and tasty there." Mr. Benette added. "When I was there with my family two years ago, my wife learnt some good cooking from the locals, and till date she enjoys cooking with those spices."

"I wonder how safe after all it will be to stay amongst the locals there?" A young officer sounded doubtful, and reflected my thoughts.

"The major issues of this country are lack of literacy and awareness about hygiene. This eventually gives birth to various social issues, but that certainly does not make India a bad country to live in."

It appeared to be a mission impossible, to leave comforts of the home country and land up in a mystic subcontinent to perform our duties.

I had moments of nervousness while thinking about Martha and children who were separated from me. In those moments, tears would fill my eyes. When would I see them again?

The days passed, and gradually turned into a month, and then next month, without much happening.

Our ship had its few stops en route, but we were advised not to step out of the ship, so it was difficult to find out much about the countries we were passing by.

It was the same group of people that I greeted either in the morning or while meeting them during breakfast, lunch and dinner. By now I had known more or less each one's life-story, or got at least the basic information. Nothing remained to be asked or discussed further.

Even the quietest of the officers had began to participate in the conversations on the ship, before the month came to an end.

We had about two more months to spend before we saw the shores of India. Like everyone else aboard, I was getting used to the situation gradually, nonetheless, waiting eagerly to reach our destination.

Fortunately, it was after 75 days that we set our sights on shores of the Indian subcontinent. That was considered a good time coverage, and a very safe sea travel.

On touching the shores, there was a sense of relief on every traveller's face, even though with an uncertainty of the experiences that awaited us in this unfamiliar land.

We reached Bombay, which is one of the biggest cities situated on the Western Coast of India.

My collegues were soon received by the British or Indian Officers one after the other, whereas I had to wait for an hour till someone came to receive me from the Indian Railways department.

I was standing helplessly in a corner to find any familiar, sane face with whom I could talk to about my destination.

In exasperation, I was questioning myself, "Where have I landed?" Away from my family, relatives and friends, surrounded by unfamiliar faces and an unknown culture.

While I stood on the Indian soil, a sense of depression took charge of me.

There were hundreds of noisy people everywhere, running about here and there.

After a good wait, I saw a short, wheatish Indian gentleman in his late 40s, approaching me, followed by a few more, all rushing into my direction.

This made me nervous. I swallowed. "Kirsten Saheb?" The leader asked. "Yes." I answered hastily.

"Sir, I am Khatri, the Regional Manager, Indian Railways." He seemed very excited to see me, or locate me rightly, to be precise.

Mr. Khatri immediately took charge of the situation, triumphantly making it clear that I was his guest.

Jokes apart, he looked into everything sincerely, making sure that all my luggage and hand baggage was properly taken care of by the accompanying helpers and escorted me towards the waiting carriage.

There was another group of people waiting for me there. I assumed it to be the Railways staff.

Suddenly, they started garlanding me, tied a scarf round my neck and applied a red powder on my forehead and what not. This was an unusual experience for me. It must be at least ten garlands that I was covered with in no time.

Suddenly, all the warnings by my fellow travellers on the ship seemed to be coming true. I was nearly suffocated, and if this had continued a little longer, I would have lost control, but luckily the chaos created by the reception diverted my mind from that.

Though, not being accustomed to such hospitality, I was uncomfortable initially. As I realised that they had gathered to receive only me, some kind of flattery for myself set in. I had never been rendered such a reception before in my life. I could not help remembering Mr. Johnson's words.

The triumphal arches had been raised outside in the honour of all those who had deboarded the ship. Walking through the crowd, bowing in answer to their salaams, it naturally felt like going through "One of the proudest moments of my life."

Strangely, the feeling of restlessness
turned into extreme composure.
I felt a tinge of pride - and felt very
special also.

But a blank look in their eyes got me asking questions to myself. I was keen to understand this place and the people around. They were harmless after all.

On a second thought, I realised that all the respect and hospitality showered on me was actually as part of the reception, something that I deserved as their boss, or should I say, as the representative of the strong rulers who had invaded their country.

Enjoying this special treatment extended towards me, and me alone, I eventually settled down in the Railway Guest House at the famous 'Victoria Terminus Railway Station.'

I was constantly being provided with the tea and snacks and the main meals. This was getting overwhelming.

One of the reasons being the oil content and spices in every snack and food which made it inedible at times.

Finally, I had to request Mr. Khatri to make it less spicy, and thankfully he seemed to understand my difficulty.

However, a weired fascination had taken over me about a lot of things of this country already, especially the food. India seemed to be so rich in the heritage of the spices and food varieties.

In the evening, I was shown around the resplendent 'Victoria Terminus Building' by Mr. Khatri. He was always available on call, and made sure that I was well looked after.

I could not stop praising the beautiful Railway staion and its intricate carvings and the workmanship. I secretly applauded the architect for creating such a monumental building, for a colonised country.

It was futile to explain my feelings to Khatri, about the dedication of the British, in beautifying India which was worth appreciating.

We walked around many other buildings which added immense splendour to the area. I gradually began to feel at home to be in this part of the city which spoke of grand works created by my countrymen.

There was the 'Municipal Corporation Building', next to which was the 'The Times of India Press', whose ownership was taken over in 1892 when an English journalist named Thomas Jewell Bennett along with Frank Morris Coleman acquired the company. As we walked further, we came across the magnificient building of St. Xavier's College.

The curiosity led me to enter the St. Xavier's College building, I had heard that, it was established by the German Priests in the late 1800s. What made this college so special? I was eager to know more about this institution.

I asked Khatri if we could go inside the college, to which he happily agreed and got the permission from the receptionist sitting at the entrance porch.

I thought of meeting the principal, and congratulate him for having such a grand college for the Indian students.

However, the receptionist did not reply clearly if I could meet him. As I introduced myself, he appeared to be little disturbed by my inquisitiveness.

It was none of my business to interfere in the working of the college. So we decided to leave from there.

On our way back, I asked Mr. Khatri, "Is there any problem at the college?"

Khatri was a very friendly and vocal person. In spite of his limitations with the English language, he could convey most of the information when asked.

But he too hesitated in replying to this particular question.

"Sir, hiding not good. This German College. All Priest people were into prisons inside here first World war by the British people." Though he spoke in broken English, I understood what he wanted to convey.

This was deplorable.

"Mr. Khatri, you mean the people from here were taken as prisoners? But why on earth..?"

"Sir, German working on the college staying there. They prison and taken near Pune-Khandala, they say torture and die."

"Who were they – professors, or helpers?"

"Mostly all also the Pujaris (Priests) at Christian temples inside." He meant priests, I guessed.

My excitement and awe died after hearing this. It is an irony that even if the war is fought in far away countries, its echoes and repercussions are lamented all over the world.

The British in me counter argued by saying that Khatri should not be believed completely. On the other hand, there was no reason why he would lie. Rather, the locals were the first ones to know the facts...the very first witnesses.

After this experience, I realised that it would be better to stick to my work, and looked forward to the next destination, Delhi, where I would reach in two days.

The next journey was to be from Bombay to Delhi by train, and this would take three days. For a person like me, who considered twelve hours in the train to London an undertaking, three days were really long.

*[** Being a German institute in British India, the college suffered wide repercussions during the First World War (1914–1918). Following the outbreak of the war, the German Jesuit Priests, mainly the older ones, were interned and detained in 1914 at the college villa in Khandala, where many died as POWs. However, the younger German Jesuits were repatriated in 1916.]*

It was interesting to observe the trains in India. I was to travel by the train in which the seats were arranged like a wagonette, so that no one would sit with his back to the engine.

The compartments were broad and comfortable, and only four people occupied them at night, upper berths being let down to complete the four beds.,

Nonetheless, for my travel they had kept the other three vacant, with only an assistant to help me during the journey.

Each carriage had a dressing room, and the windows had external wooden venetian shutters, to protect from the dust and the sun. Still three days and two nights, never hasting, never resting, were to me unterminable.

One only saw a flat land mile upon mile, but the masses of the people swarmed everywhere.

Every station platform was densely crowded by them.

In the small hours of the night, women rushed about with the babies in their arms, and crying children at their heels.

The men ran helter-skelter, in sheer excitement and screaming out to their friends at the Railway Station.

I honestly confess that the excessively overwhelming crowds of the people left me frightened.

We were in a distant land, I thought, not more than a handful of Europeans, and what was there to prevent these myriads from overpowering and obliterating us, as if we never existed?

There was something to prevent it, as everybody had told me on way to India, they were the most law abiding and loyal people in the world. But even then, my scepticism and fears got the better of my reason and faith.

As the train stopped at the first station in the outskirts of Delhi, a crowd of the native officials and notables joined us, their ranks swelling at each succeeding station.

Finally, when I reached Delhi, and looked out of the carriage window, there were about hundreds of them again, waiting to welcome me.

The same ritual of the garlanding, music and application of the red powder on the forehead was repeated.

I needed to begin to communicate now, or soon I would be actually suffocated.

I caught hold of the person who appeared to be a Senior Officer there, "Hello!"

He came running to me. "Please tell everyone to stop this."

"Yes, Sir, Please! Thank you!" He sounded confused and scared. "Me, Johri!"

So he was Mr. Johri, whom I had simply asked to stop all that,

"Why all this is going on again and again?"

He replied, very proudly, (in English), "Saheb, Good luck custom, welcome you - and - always this safety to you so God give. We wish good for you not fall sick."

I was embarrassed.

In spite of his broken English, I could gather the gist of the matter.

Here, I was representing myself as a foreign invader, and they were praying for my well being. I couldn't say anything further.

A carriage took me to the house that I was supposed to be staying in, for the time being.

It was a decent house with a fleet of attendants to look after me.

Mr Khatri, had sent a welcome team to receive me, and they immediately took charge of my belongings and tried to make me feel comfortable.

This was very reassuring.

They took me in a carriage to the area where many British Officers lived.

I descended to enter a sprawling bunglow, tastefully built, by the previous occupants, whom I guessed to be my countrymen.

Did all this make us feel more at home in a foreign land? This question was not easy to answer.

But it was very important for me not to regret for what I was in, rather enjoy the experiences.

Gradually it dawned upon me that the life I had anticipated to be in India was based mostly on my fears and reality was perhaps more pleasant.

Initially, I used to feel like an alien here, and it was a constant battle to gather all my energy and keep calm as every new day began. Everything was so different here.

Starting from dressing style of the people, to the language they spoke (they called it Hindustani or Hindi) we were a world apart. Soon I observed that the educated, and the elite were all the time trying to imitate our style of dressing, ways of living, our food and every area of life to be called at par with the British. This was interesting and amusing.

Many such observations helped me to settle mentally to begin with, and in turn, if not enjoy, at least respect their efforts to make me comfortable. I started trying to be a part of their system.

It was getting simpler and easier as the days passed by. I also realised that in fact, my lifestyle in India was a luxurious one within the limited means.

I had the helpers who constantly looked after my smallest needs throughout the day. But on the other hand, there was hardly anything else that one would look forward to other than work.

It is impossible to narrate in a few words about how I felt to be living in an Indian environment when I considered living with my family here.

I shuddered at the thought of Martha coming here and managing without any proper framework of things.

The Anglo-Indian housekeeping was too bewildered to say anything, as the aspect of everything was very different from what it was at home.

Individually, we were like the migratory birds of India, and had to build our nests with whatever material we could find.

The result was not bad, considering the complete absence of home appliances or skilled labour.

The houses were adapted according to the climate, and perhaps Martha too would get accustomed to living in this system once she was here.

The house was square in shape, one storied, flat-roofed, with a pillared verandah on each side, five rooms, three in a row, without an entrance or any passage, each room opening into the other, and having one or two doors and windows into the bargain.

'Here rooms have a thousand doors, and at home just one'.

So many doors and windows are a blessing in summer, but not appreciated in the winters.

Considering that if the house was furnished with draperies, pictures and curtains, it would have a different look altogether, but unfortunately, that was not going to happen here.

With its high ceiling and the folding doors, the house looked more like a church.

Every bedroom had a bathroom attached, but it was a low wall separating it in one corner, and drainage was but a small hole in one corner.

There was no pantry like home, though cooking was to be done by my khansama- (cook) provided by the railways.

The kitchen was a dark little room, with a board on the mud floor to hold the raw food, two tumbled-down bricks in one corner, a stone receptacle to throw the water, which was drained out through a hole in the wall.

My servants lived in a group of small, detached houses.

Whenever I wanted some help, an orderly, who always sat in the verandah, went to call any one of the seven servants.

There of course, was no bell in the house, so it was only through loud calls and shouts that messages were conveyed and replied whenever needed.

The servants included the khansama, waterman, sweeper, milkman, and house servants.

Funnily, no servant other than the cook had a defined work.

Everyone did every work, and I did not much bother, as far as my office routine was set well.

With so many servants at my disposal, there was no situation where I needed to be rude or overpowering towards the locals that worked for me. Ironically, they appeared to be considering us next to Gods.

I was happy with this arrangement, though my conscious did not agree with this. A lot more can be written about this, but alas, the system established did not allow them even to think beyond their existence of this sort.

All the servants were very honest, ever ready to help, take my orders and to fulfil them happily.

My orderly, Ajitsingh, would be there all the time, Khansama- Dariya, would prepare breakfast including eggs, tea, milk etc. Ajitsingh would serve it to me and once I was ready to leave for the office, he would accompany me throughout the day, looking after every small detail that I might ask for.

I had started enjoying the Indian food that my cook used to prepare for me, especially the chicken varieties.

I later learnt that North India was famous for its non-vegetarian preparations, and I wanted Martha to learn these recepies some day.

It was natural that Martha would not be able to imagine what type of life I lived here.

When I had left London, she was worried that I would fall sick or would have an accident with animals, since elephants or camels were assumed to be moving on the roads. Now that I had started living here, this humoured me a lot.

Talking about my work, which was of prime importance for me, there was no time to be wasted after reaching Delhi, and hence I started with my work, the assignment for which I had travelled thousands of miles.

It was the month of June now, a real warm time here. Though I had started enjoying it, compared to the bitter cold of London.

Strangely, even this city had unexpected showers at odd hours though not as frequently as in London, but nonetheless, made the atmosphere cooler, and it was certainly welcome.

I used to start my day early at the office working on some important projects. One major project was preparing the budget for the Indian Railways. Since I was in Delhi, all the provinces under the British Government had to be covered by me.

The Railway budget had to be segregated from the overall budget of the country, that was being implemented so far, and had to be presented at the Parliament, as well as to His Excellency Sir Viceroy by next September. It was inevitable that this prime project was completed as soon as possible.

There were hundreds of employees and many experts working upon it day and night. Looking at the overall picture, I was proud of my fellow countrymen who had taken up such an assignment for the country that was merely colonised.

However, the work left little time for my relaxation and recreation.

But whenever I was free, I used to spend time at Mr. Kellog and Mr. Smith's house after office hours, who were also deputed at Delhi as the Government officers for Civil works. They had their families here, and meeting them made me forget the pains of living away from my family.

We regularly met to play tennis or golf, and to dine together atleast once a week. More often it was them calling me over. Whenever I invited them, my khansama cooked his speciality of chicken, which he excelled at.

I exchanged notes regularly with these two families that come and go with books, home newspapers, flowers, fruits and games etc.

However, despite of all our efforts, things which were dear to us were entirely absent here.

There was no stir in the politics to rouse the fighting spirit or the pictures to delight the eyes. Not to mention the bread and vegetables in varied tastes and recipes, and the delicious milk that was served as part of breakfast in the morning.

I used to write long letters to Martha, initially once a week after reaching India. I missed her and both my children Jane and Joshua very much. I also made sure to mention that it was not as bad as she had imagined.

Initially, Martha must have thought that I was giving her all wrong information, but as my letters to her and the children sounded more pleasant each time, maybe she was convinced and felt peaceful.

Martha had started replying to my long letters, with longer answers, explaining how she was getting used to my absence, but for children it was difficult. They missed their Papa. These letters always brought tears to my eyes.

Eventually, as I settled down, the frequency of my letters to England reduced to once a month, and later to once in two months. I did not realise this, and even if I did, could do nothing about it due to increase in the workload. Martha continued to write to me with the same fervour and regularity, however busy I might be, I waited eagerly for her letters.

I learnt a lot while working on the huge project of the constantly increasing network of the Railways in India. Railway was a commodity in India which was well established already, with a lot of efforts put in by the British Government, and the network was spreading very fast. It was indeed one of the proudest possesions for us.

Between 1860 and 1880, the Indian Railway network grew from 838 miles to 15,842 miles in India, making the train ticket a highly desired commodity for a young entrepreneur.

The impetus given to commerce by the multiplied means of communication taken up as a task by the Englishmen had unquestionably brought material prosperity to this country.

As a result, any possibility of the people being overtaken by a drought or a famine in India were reduced greatly. Formerly, the only means of sending grains mainly to a tract afflicted by the scarcity was by the slow caravans of laden camels or bullock carts.

People who knew the history of Madras famine in 1877-78, could understand value of the railways, through which the grain was brought from granaries in more fortunate districts, to the millions who without it would have most certainly died.

Indian Railways was helpful for all the people in their days of prosperity and in the hours of need as well. Besides, it had strengthened the empire in another quarter, where a weakness would result in the British India disappearing from the map of the world.

It was a great foresight of the Government in developing the railways here. All our great cantonments, all our fortresses and arsenals, were now connected with each other, and with the seaboard, through the railways, due to which, strength of the European troops for action in or out of the borders of the British India had increased enormously.

'An Indian Railway Station, wrote Dr. Norman Macleod in 1871, is unique, as affording and easy study of the native races and the customs.'

There were many officers like me in Delhi, working and compiling the Railways' reports, assessing them, segregating them and suggesting various means for making it more functional and more simplified. Thus, we worked as a team there, and it was a comfortable environment, hardly realising the absence of not being in London.

I was quite settled after spending about four months in now much familiar Delhi, when I received a wire from the London Head Office to start my work in Lucknow as part of the completion of the project.

While working in Delhi, I did not have to deal much with the Indian employees directly, on one-on-one level. This would not be the case in Lucknow, where I would have to deal directly with the employees, and this made me nervous once again. Similar to my feeling on descending at the Bombay port a few months ago. Lucknow was an important city of the United Provinces. It was a major Railway Junction. Besides, a grand Railway Station was being built there somewhere at the area known as Charbaug.

The importance of that project and the completion of the Budget required me to be stationed there now onwards.

Lucknow was a much smaller city – a town to be precise- compared to Delhi, but the lifestyle was similar, and the weather cooler. It was more towards the north of India, on the banks of the river Gomati.

I had heard about Lucknow from my friends in Delhi that it was more of a heritage city where the kings, Navabs and the rulers were known for their cultural inheritance and tastes. This interested me and I was looking forward to this as I reached there the next week.

I observed that people were very friendly there and very ethical. They never ever cheated on others, in the areas of business and daily lives. At the same time, a clan of people called themselves 'Navabi' – which meant 'King-like'. Perhaps this was a reflection of their past glory of this wonderful place. Indeed they meant no harm or intended non-cooperation of any kind.

At the Lucknow Railway office, around 100 employees worked under me. Much to my relief, each one of them, was a dedicated and sincere employee, so that I had no difficulty in dealing with the staff at various levels. Perhaps they competed among themselves only to impress me many a times, which was sad.

Of all the employees, one management trainee, who was now a permanent employee drew my attention soon. His name was Mukund Pandey.

It was after a month of my joining the office that Mukund had returned from his marriage leave. He had brought a packet of sweets for me. I appreciated his gesture.

I soon observed his dedication towards work and the faithfulness towards the British, which was impressive. I had never seen him interact much with the other employees in the office or be part of the internal politics. His entire focus used to be on the work assigned to him.

As the time passed, I saw that Mukund was always eager to please me, by completing the assignments with sincerity and efficiency.

I did not have many friends in Lucknow as I had in Delhi, hence I used to often converse with him, and learn more about the world that I was in.

Mukund always talked to me with extreme enthusiasm, and shared stories about his wife Leela and parents who lived with him.

Sometimes, he used to invite me to his house for meals in the evening. In fact, very often I was invited by few other employees as well. This was a very pleasant experience for me and I enjoyed the hospitality and delicious food, though having a very different taste of India.

September 1924 saw the arrival of His Majesty Sir Viceroy to India, especially to attend the meeting at Shimla, which was to discuss the separation of the Indian Railways Budget from the main Budget of the country.

I was the fortunate one to attend this meeting, representing the United Provinces worksheets and the performance at the meeting. The meeting was very successful and our work was praised by His Majesty the King, and in turn everyone congratulated me for my good work.

*[**Some of the major works discussed were as follows:*

The key recommendations are as follows: Separation of Railway Finances:

Complete separation of the Railway budget from the general budget of the country has to be done. Its reconstruction was done in a form which frees the great commercial business from the trammels of a system which assumes that the concern goes out of business on every 31st of March and recommences de novo (from the beginning) on the 1st of April. The general revenues are to receive a definite annual contribution from the Railways which would be the first charge on the net receipts of the Railways.

Emancipation of Railway Management:

The Railway Management's emancipation from the control of the Finance Department is recommended.

Equalisation of Dividends:

The committee recommends that a Depreciation Fund and Railway Reserves be built so that the dividends may be equalised. A system of finance is being introduced to have an unimpaired control of the House while ensuring the general revenues a fair returnfrom their Railway property, more suited to the needs of a vast commercial undertaking.

Loan Account Separation:

Separation of the Loan Account (known as capital-at-charge) and the Block Account (gross block of assets) followed in the wake of separation of the Railway Finance. The term the Capital Outlay in the statistical reports is being changed to the capital-at- charge. The contribution will be based on the Capital-at-Charge and working results of the commercial lines which will be the sum equal to one per cent on the capital-at- charge.

Borrowings of the Railways:

The Railway administration will subject to the conditions prescribed by the Government of India, to borrow temporarily from the capital, or from the reserve to cater to the ensuing expenditure if there is a lack of the funds. Such loans have to be repaid if taken from the revenue budget of the years to come.

A Standing Finance Committee for Railways:

The Department of Railways will submit its estimates to the newly constituted State Finance Commission before it is time for the deliberation on the demand for grants for the Railways. It is further recommended that expenditure maybe shown under a new and separate depreciation fund.

Budget Presentation:

The Railway budget is to be presented to the Legislature prior to the general budget within the distinct days for its discussion. The accounts and functions of the Railways would be stated by the Member-in-Charge.

Periodic Revision

These recommendations will be tested for at least three years and then revised from time to time. Hence, the Railway budget is being separated from the general budget to mark a new phase in the Indian Financial Administration.]

I observed that all the employees worked industriously during the preparation of these reports with Mukund toiling with more perseverance and dedication.

It was now time for me to revert to Delhi. I had also heard from some of my colleagues that I might be called back to London, since the things were not running very smoothly there as far as the American project was concerned.

In consideration of my leaving Lucknow, I was asked to nominate the next officer who would replace me to take charge of the Lucknow Railway office.

Though the hierarchy did not allow, I recommended Mukund's name for it, as I was sure that he would carry out the responsibilities well with the kind of passion and abilities he possessed.

After some contemplations and the questions asked from Mukund, he was selected for the post. Though this post was not exactly of the Head of United Provinces, it did give a lot of power to him.

An English Police officer from Lucknow, Mr. Sinha, did raise an objection to my nominating Mukund for this post. He claimed that Mukund's family consisted of the revolutionaries and rebelled against the British Government.

I did not pay any heed to this or encouraged the objection, since it would be unfair not to value his good work, who was in fact doing a good job for the British Government.

I left for Delhi in the beginning of 1925, with a heavy heart, leaving behind my friend Mukund to take charge. The small city of Lucknow had won me over in many ways, especially the warmth and the hospitality that I enjoyed there. I was given a very special farewell by the Railway employees on the last day.

After a very short stay at Delhi, within a month, I was asked to return to London.

I was exhilarated to hear the news. My work was immensely praised at the H.O. and I was promoted to a very senior post in the London office. I was likely to take the position of Mr. Tumbleton, as he was being transferred to another department there.

I also heard rumours that I was to be felicitated as well as to be sent to America for the Railway Project there. My dream to visit USA was about to come true. This time I had decided to take Martha and children along with me. We had truly lived too long without each other, and I missed them badly.

I sailed for London on 5th July, 1925 and reached the shores of London by the last week of September. I was meeting my family after two years. The children had grown up, and Martha looked tired now. I felt very touched to meet them, and deeply sorry for the state of things we had to go through, just to present ourselves at the other end of the world.

No one would understand the silent sacrifices that each family goes through in the power dynamics in the process of the colonisation.

It was already about six months that I had returned from India, when I came across the news of a shocking train robbery in Kakori near Lucknow while going through the course of events in India. More shocking were the names involved in the robbery, and my heart missed a beat to read that Mukund Gupta, a chief Railways' Officer was involved in the robbery. A tear dropped down from my eyes as all the memories of Lucknow were revived in a span of a few minutes.

I started following up on this case, its entire hearings and the judgement eventually.

Somehow, I could never digest the judgement rendered by the British Court in this case.

How I wish I was in India to help the innocent! This regret stayed with me all my life.

❑

5

Kakori Train Robbery Takes Shape

Banvari Narrates

As the Jailor Saheb read out names of the prisoners to be released from the Lucknow Central Jail after the morning round on Monday, all the eyes and ears were attentive towards what was to follow.

I was supposed to be in the jail for 3 months as per the court orders, but my sentence would complete after 6 months, i.e., next week. There was no sign of my release, along with many of other jailmates.

And I was desperate to return home.

During the days of my imprisonment, Biru used to visit me, accompanied by Pitaji at times. Initially, they used to visit me frequently. As the time passed, their visits tapered down, although I was being updated with all the developements at home.

Almost immediately after I was jailed, Satish had left home to join the revolutionaries. His impulsive decision had disturbed me greatly. I wished he could have waited till I returned.

One thing, however, was worth feeling happy about, Leela's marriage was fixed with Bagga's friend, Mukund Pandey.

This sounded like Bagga's idea, but on the second thought, I felt that it was a wise decision. Leela's future life would be happy, as Mukund would prove to be a good husband for her.

He had secured good marks in final B.A. exams and was likely to secure a decent job. Another factor being his faith in the British Government.

Strange, how the values which we do not favour or agree with, become a reason for the support to our family.

It would also be good for Pitaji and Mataji, if Mukund became their son-in-law. With Mukund's modest background his family would always look up to our family.

So next time when I meet Mukund, I would meet him as my brother-in-law.

My train of thoughts was interrupted when I heard my name being called out, 'Banvari Gupta' along with few other names.

I could not believe it at first. But yes, I was free now.

A prison officer opened the door of my cell after some time.

There were many friends who had already been released with me, where as some were still in the jail to bid me goodbye.

I realised that I had developed a good friendship with everyone during my stay in the jail. Many of them were already in the various revolutionary groups from the 'Famous Four'- Delhi, Allahabad, Lucknow and Kanpur, whereas a few were victims of their attempt to do something good for the country's freedom.

As I put on my old clothes, a sense of freedom prevailed upon me.

After experiencing a long hospitality of the jail, today I was returning home.

Biru had often visited the jail to inquire about my release. I wondered if he would be waiting today at the main gate to receive me.

As I stepped out in the daylight, climbing up the stairs towards the free world, indeed, Biru was waiting for me.

"Uncle!" He shouted delightfully and came running towards me and hugged me.

I must have looked like a zombie with uneven, roughly grown beard and hair in disarray, and wearing clothes that I had last worn, more than two hundred days ago.

"Biru! How are you? How is everyone at home?" I could barely speak. My throat choked with emotions and speech failed me.

Biru caught my hand and took me aside. He had brought home- made Halwa (sweet) prepared by Mataji to celebrate my release from the jail.

"Do you know Uncle? This is my fourth visit to the jail to find out if you are released. Everyone is eagerly waiting for you at home." Though I am not a person of emotions, a few tears dropped down from my eyes today.

Biru had booked a tonga to take me home.

I felt as if the road was not coming to an end. Finally, we reached home. I hurriedly opened the door of my house.

Mataji was waiting for me. It appeared as though she had been sitting there since the day I was jailed.

Pitaji was not at home, with an excuse of some urgent work. He would be too emotional to see me return.

> *"Kaise ho beta?"(How are you, son?) Mataji hugged me, as I touched her feet. She welcomed me with a diya (earthen lamp with a burning wick soaked in ghee) in a thaali (plate) and sung aarti (religious hymns).*
>
> *Leela came to me and held my hand. "Banvari Bhaiya, Welcome home! We missed you so much."*

The warm welcome and hearty reception made me fully alive after a long stay in the jail. Undoubtedly, home has a different comfort feeling, physically and emotionally.

The food was ready, we sat down together for lunch.

After surviving somehow on the stinking food which the prisoners were given in the jail, I was eating the soulful food prepared by Mataji. I had no courage to share my experiences with her about the Jail food.

Hence without showing much excitement or getting emotional, I fed myself fully upto the brim.

I felt Bagga's absence in the house acutely. "Mataji, Is Leela getting married?"

"Yes beta, (son) this proposal seems good for her. She is very happy. Mukund Kumar takes good care of Leela, me and your Pitaji." She muttered softly, "After all, he is the one we all are dependent on, you know."

> *I nodded. I did not have anything against Mukund, except that our ideologies had never coincided, but I guess that looking at the situation, it was the only safe way out for the well being and happiness of my family.*

It was clear that the British Police was ruthless. Sooner or later, they would reach for me as well as Bagga.

I was very eager to know more about Bagga and his decision to leave home so abruptly. I wanted to know what happened to him, but who could tell me about him? Maybe Mukund or Leela? I should go and meet Mukund.

Yes, I decided to go and meet him the next day.

A good bath and home food was like experiencing heaven. At last, the nightmare was cleared from my system, I was sitting with Mataji again. I was her first son, born after my late sisters, and we both shared a different and special bond.

Mataji often used to open her heart to me during my growing years. She liked to confide in me, even her worries and problems.

I could feel that she must have waited for these moments ever since I was imprisoned.

"Mataji! How are you?" She smiled through her tears. "I am okay my son."

"You look thinner and tired." I always pampered her. "Now that I am back, you need not worry. I will take care of everything. Pitaji should also relax now."

Mataji drew a deep breath. "Let us hope so, son. Leela's marriage is finalised, and it is a happy event for all of us. Since you are back now, both of us are greatly relieved."

This embarrassed me, realising about negligence towards my duties for the family, I decided to invest all my energy into the preparations and be helpful to m y parents now onwards.

"So what if Bagga is not at home, I will take charge of all the responsibilities. You do not have to worry," and hugged to comfort her.

Ma was happy, we felt that things had started falling in place once again.

Unfortunately, this did not last for long. The destiny had already decided something else for me.

This happened after about a week of my release. I was relaxing in the afternoon when Bholu, Lalaji Paanwala's messenger brought a chit for me.

It read, "Naya paan khane aao" (Come to eat a new betel leaf).

I was very curious to find out what was happening with my team, and within ten minutes, left to see Lalaji.

When I reached Lalaji's shop, I saw a familiar person waiting for me at some distance.

A highly respected leader of our group, a brilliant and shrewd organiser, Shachindra Nath Bakshi, known as Prabhas to everyone, was waiting under a tree.

He signalled me to follow him, and soon we reached a deserted area on the banks of the Gomti river. It was early evening, and the darkness was yet to set in. Making sure that no one was following us, we started talking in a quiet corner.

Prabhas and everyone in our team knew about my imprisonment.

I briefly narrated my experiences in the jail and the unfair and prejudiced treatment given to the political prisoners there. He seemed disturbed to hear my story. "Yes, we are somewhat aware of this. Something will have to be done. I will convey this to Avdhutji and Panditji." He murmured. He was also upset to hear the manner in which the pamphlet throwing case was handled and my imprisonment was extended indefinitely.

But the information he shared was highly alarming for me.

He told me about a dangerous detective posted in the Union Provinces, who was after the lives of the revolutionaries.

"As you must be knowing, there is a clan of people who work as CIDs to keep track of the revolutionaries. They have weird and brutal ways to torture and dictate their lives. We, the freedom fighters, possess such mettle that they (CIDs) often fail to dampen our spirits. So it's not every time they are fortunate enough to victimise us to their inhumanity. One such dangerous person is Rai Bahadur Jitendra Nath Chatterji. He is a detective working for the British Government. He was honoured as 'Rai Bahadur' for his incessant and faithful work for the Government, and now he heads the group of detectives who work for the British."

He continued, "He is notorious in finding and getting information about the revolutionaries and their movements. He identified many fighters and got them jailed with the help of the Police and other spies who were part of the Anushilan Samiti founded by Satish Chandra Basu, (purpose: Indian independence and motto: united India), when he was in Eastern Bengal. Needless to say, that those who were jailed underwent a prolonged torturous life of confinement. Thus, his name was recommended even by the High Command of the British. He went on, "During the phase of shifting of the British capital from Calcutta to Delhi in the year 1911, many unexpected incidents followed."

Shachin da (Prabhas) paused. "As you are aware, there was an attempt to assassinate the Viceroy of

India, Lord Harding, when the British Government realised two important points.

Firstly, the United Provinces were turning dangerous for the British Government, and secondly, there was a dire need to find the trails of the revolutionaries there. Under these circumstances, Rai Bahadur's name was suggested and he was shifted to Benaras to spy against the revolutionary activities. He used to work as the Principal of a school in Eastern Bengal. For the new assignment, the Government tempted him to go to Benaras offering him designation of the Principal of a school in Benaras, with his past services added to his credit. Besides, he was being nominated a detective for the whole Jila (district), where he could use the provided funds as per his wish, and no questions would be asked since he was being selected for this special job as an officer working for the British Government. No one could have denied this offer, obviously it did melt Rai Bahadur as well." Taking a deep breath, Shachin da continued,

"Unfortunately, he is here in Lucknow now. Hope you do not confront him."

I was dumbstruck to hear this story and could only say, "He will certainly keep track of me, Prabhas, now that I am released from the jail."

Shachin da smiled and patted me on the back. "I am here to help you. My mission is to follow him, as he has ruined the lives of many of our groupmates, and the innocent boys too. Will talk about it some other time, but in the meanwhile you do take care. Do not get into any controversy."

I said, "Yes!" and nodded in despair.

In a few days of my release from the jail, there was some eagle-eyed rival eagerly awaiting to trap me again.

"By the way, your brother is doing very well."

The mention of Bagga, lit up my face. "Where is he, Prabhas? I haven't met him since the last six months."

"Do not worry about him. He is a brave boy. He is very clever and understands the nitty gritties of our plans. Avdhutji and Captain regard him immensely. At present he is in Benaras. I am going there soon, and will convey your message. I must leave now." We bid good bye to each other, promising to keep the track of whatever happened at our ends.

Shachindra Nath Bakshi was the son of a rich lawyer, originally from Calcutta, who had settled in Delhi. Unlike his father who was dedicated and loyal towards the British, the passionately patriotic Shachin da had joined the revolutionary group, and was a promising leader as well as the brain behind many of our important missions.

After this important meeting, I reached home late in the evening still thinking about my conversation with Prabhas.

Everyone was waiting for me including Pitaji, Leela and Mukund along with Mataji.

I entered the house and bowed to touch Pitaji's feet. Though I had met him during the week, today I found him sitting peacefully in his easy chair near the window. He was in tears to see me come home, and couldn't speak anything.

Mukund hugged me. I liked his gesture. I also felt greatly relieved. The nagging worry about my family's safety and care in Bagga's and my absence as if flew into the air. Mukund was there as a big and reliable pillar of support.

After the usual talk, there was nothing much to discuss regarding my return or future plans, about which I myself did not know anything. Moreover, such issues were not worth discussing in the family gathering. Naturally, the conversation turned towards Leela and Mukund's marriage. They both were very excited about the forthcoming functions and narrated to me how the celebrations were planned.

I missed my younger brother all of a sudden. I had known all along that he would choose the path of fighting for the country's freedom. But why leave the house so suddenly?

Later all of us had dinner together, and I felt very comfortable to see Mukund becoming the part of our family soon. When Mukund was leaving, I asked him casually, "Did you meet Bagga anytime?"

Mukund looked pained to answer my question. He evaded looking into my eyes, and offered a lame reply instead. "Biru gets his news often. I have not met him since he left. Now that I am busy with my work and marriage preparations, I don't get time as well."

This surprised and disappointed me. Why was Mukund so defensive in talking about Bagga, who was his best friend not so long ago? Besides, he was going to be the part of our family soon. Was it because both had ideologically parted their ways or was it something else?

It was futile to ask him anything further.

I looked at Leela, who was looking down all this while. I had known my sister since her birth, and could vouch for her cleverness and wisdom. I decided to talk to her later.

The next morning, I was wondering about Bagga and the detective that Prabhas had warned me about.

It was vital for me to find out how much the detective supreme knew about us and our family.

Leela entered my room with a cup of freshly prepared tea. It was like back to old times, and this was a long-forgotten luxury for me.

"Muniya, I missed these luxuries in jail."

Leela smiled happily, though there was some pain added to it.

Returning home from the jail was full of surprises for me, and one more was added by Leela.

Before I could say anything further, Leela closed the door behind her.

"What is the matter?" I was surprised. What information she wanted to share with me?

"Bhaiya, there is something important I want to tell you about." My youngest sister had really grown up.

I looked at her proudly. "Yes, Leela, please speak freely."

Leela sat opposite me on a chair and in a hushed tone started talking, "A few months back, Bagga Bhaiya came home to meet me at night secretly when Mataji and Pitaji were asleep. I was overwhelmed to see him. I spoke in whispers, lest I should wake up someone, I offered him some laddoos I had prepared that day. Bagga Bhaiya picked up a laddoo and ate it fondly. He picked up two more and then sat down. He was in tears. He said that as a brother I should be giving you gifts, but look at me, I am eating the laddoos."

I said, "Bhaiya! Please do not think like this. I can do anything for you."

Bagga Bhaiya then said, "Leela, I need your help." I was surprised. How could I be of any help to him?

He took me to the backyard and asked, "Muniya, how are you? I hope you are happy to marry my friend Mukund?"

"Yes, Bhaiya, you have been so kind. He is a nice person who can look after both Mataji and Pitaji besides me, in your and Banvari Bhaiya's absence."

"Leela, can you do me a favour?" He stopped, hesitating to speak. I encouraged him, "Of course Bhaiya."

> *"Okay! Listen carefully. You will soon start receiving some posts which will come in your name from the various parts of India. You will be my post box. You will have to pass on those posts to Lalaji, or Agarwalji without opening."*

This was going to be difficult. "I had to receive the posts when no one was noticing. But it was going to help my brother and my country, therefore obviously I did not refuse. Hence, I have been doing this regularly for a few months now."

I was touched and impressed by Leela's courage. My little, frail sister was helping the freedom fighters.

I got up and put my hand over Leela's head and blessed her.

"Muniya, you are a brave girl. No one would take such a risk."

Leela replied, "I have seen you and Bagga Bhaiya both ready to do anything for the country's freedom. Can't I do even this much?"

This was getting very emotional. Soon Leela will get married and go to live with her husband and in-laws.

I decided to go out and meet Lalaji. Suddenly, I heard some people talking in the main hall of our house. I thought it might be some friend of Pitaji who had come to visit us.

As I tried to peep into the room, Pitaji called me. "Banvari, come meet my old friend."

It was imperative that I go and meet Uncle. I greeted and bowed to him, and sat down at a little distance. "He is Rai Bahadur Jiterndra Nath Chatterji, a very renowned Government officer."

I was aghast!

It was only yesterday that Shachin da had warned me about him. Thank God! I was cautioned in time.

I detested this person as soon as I set my eyes on him. I realised that I had to play my cards carefully.

"Namaste Uncle! I am very happy to see that you have come to visit us."

Rai Bahadur looked at me and smiled. "Yes, I always feel happy to meet my old friends and their children. What are your career plans after the exams?"

This was a trap. A wrong answer would put not only me, but my family also in deep waters.

'Sir, I could not appear for all the exams due to health issues. At the time of my second exam paper I fell ill, so I took a drop this time.'

Rai Bahadur smiled and said with a nod, "Good decision."

After a few minutes of casual talk, I excused myself, "Uncle, excuse me. I need to go."

Rai Bahadur said, "Of course! Go ahead! See you and your brother soon."

This man was certainly dangerous.

I rushed out of the house and waited at the corner to find out more about Rai Bahadur's plans. In less than five minutes, he too came out and started looking around. It was obvious that he was searching for me and was trying to follow me.

I decided that it was best to avoid him at present, and tell everything to Shachin da first who can help me tackle this menace.

As the night drew closer, I went to Lalaji and conveyed in short about the danger looming over me, and requested him to update Prabhas about it.

Lalaji tried to pacify me by saying that I should have patience, since Shachin da was soon to return from Benaras by the weekend.

Relieved by Lalaji's words, I decided to take it easy for the next few days.

On Sunday morning, I was sitting at a chai shop, enjoying the freedom and feeling relaxed. I was also wondering about what my next action should be, when I was jolted to see someone coming towards me. It was Rai Bahadur himself.

Unfortunately, with a cup of tea in my hand, it was difficult to run away from there or hide my face. I desperately tried to keep a strong facade.

Smilingly Rai Bahadur sat next to me. "Son, (bete) a very few good boys like you are to be found in today's society."

This was an unexpected move. Well done, old devil!

"Thank you Uncle! Please tell me what I can do for you?"

Rai Bahadur was waiting for this, I guess. He turned towards me and looking straight into my eyes he said, "I am sure you would like to settle down sooner or later in life, and marry a good girl."

What nonsense was this? Marriage? He wishes me to get married?

I stammered, and to protect myself, out of desperation I leaked an important information, "Uncle, let me clear my exams, besides my sister is getting married next month."

This gave him a stronger reason to go on.

"Of course, I understand how parents are worried to get their daughters married off. So is my sister." He sighed.

"My sister's daughter is in her teens, and I feel that you are a good match for her. I am certain that you will keep her very happy."

Shachin da was right! This Rai Bahadur fellow knew all the ways to exhaust one's patience.

Alas! Unfortunately, I was stuck with him now and could notfind a way to get out. Much to my exasperation, Rai Bahadur continued to lecture me on the advantages of getting married and settling down in life for the next fifteen minutes.

"So, when do we meet your future wife and visit my sister's place in Allahabad?"

This was like the last straw on the camel's back.

"Sir, I have other plans." I could not tolerate one more word from him.

"Dekho, (see) you will get some dahej (dowry) as well. And of course, that can be useful to you and your parents for your sister's marriage. Let me add that my sister's family is well-known in Allahabad, which will make your parents proud."

It would be best to ignore this verbal onslaught and leave, I told myself. As I tried to get up, Rai Bahadur grabbed my hand and pulled me back to the seat.

This was the limit. I could not endure this any further.

Softly uttering a few gaalis (abuses) in chaste Hindi, I spoke loudly, "Uncle, shaadi ki aisi ki taisi, maine to desh ki azadi se shaadi kar li hai." (Forget about marriage, I have married to the freedom of my country!).

Saying this, I pulled myself away from Rai Bahadur and returned home almost running.

On second thoughts, I wish I had turned back to see the angered and ashen face of that arrogant traitor which would have made many of my groupmates go into splits of laughter.

My only regret was if I should have learnt some more tips from Shachin da in anticipation to protect myself. But it was too late now.

This scum of the country had read my mind and forced me to speak up my thoughts in exasperation.

For the next few days, I was feeling lost, since my anger and resentment knew no bounds. I was helpless without Shachin da, and I had to wait for two more days before he returned from Benaras.

On Wednesday, I decided that I must at least convey to Lalaji about my encounter with Rai Bahadur.

Before I could leave the house, there was a knock at the door.

Much to my bewilderment, it was a Policeman. "What is the matter, Officer?"

"Are you Banvari Gupta?" He asked. I said "Yes, Sir!" "You are supposed to report at the police station."

"But officer, why should I? I have been released from the jail only last week."

"Exactly. There is a complaint pending against you from the Central jail. Do not worry. You will be released if you are found innocent."

This did not sound normal. I replied "Okay, give me five minutes."

I went inside the house, and called Leela. "Muniya, there seems to be some problem. I have been called at the police station. If anything happens, go to Lalaji's shop and tell him to give this chit to Prabhas. He will do the needful."

Rai Bahadur's claws seemed to have spread at various levels, but it was meaningless to fight or do anything against him at that moment.

Soon I was taken to the main Police Station of Lucknow, and was immediately taken into the custody without any questions or formalities, or notice or slightest indication was also not provided by the old monstor.

Though, I tried to argue with the Prison Officer by asking questions and proving my innocence, I was completely ignored.

What a turn of events! Only one weak moment saw me again among my old comrades in the same jail within less than a fortnight.

Alas! I wish I was more careful and attentive to what Shachin da was trying to hint at.

Much to my misfortune, I could neither attend Leela and Mukund's marriage, nor be of any help to my family now.

Mukund Narrates

It was Saturday, 8th December 1924. I was about to leave for the office, and looked for Leela to say 'Bye' to her but she could not be seen anywhere.

That worried me. I went to the backyard, where she was pulling water from the well. There she was! She appeared exhausted, and looked pale too.

I was concerned. Putting my office bag aside, I ran to her.

Holding her hand, I said, "Leela! Why don't you take care of your health? We have Shambhu to help you, who can do all this work. Please don't strain yourself."

As I held her in my arms, suddenly she fainted.

I panicked and started shouting, "Mataji! Pitaji! Something has happened to Leela!" Mataji immediately came running.

As she saw Leela fainting, Mataji rushed to the kitchen and got some jeera (caraway seeds), which was considered to be an immediate treatment for such symptoms.

In two minutes Leela recovered, but was still very weak and sat down on the floor.

Looking at Leela's health, I was doubtful about going for work today.

With the help of Shambhu and Biru, I brought her to the bedroom. As she was relaxed now, I decided to request for a casual leave at the office.

However, in the times of no communicative media, it was imperative that I should go to office to ask for a leave myself, or convey through any of the colleagues. It was my good fortune that looking at my situation, Kirstein Sahib would not reject my request for a leave today.

Finding a simpler way out, I went to Ram Singh Ji Rastogi's house who lived a little away from my house and on the way to the Railways' Office.

Rastogi Ji was an Accountant at the Railways' office, and we worked together frequently as a team on different projects. I had helped him understand the concept of the Balance Sheet, and so on and so forth.

I hurried to his house, and luckily, before Mr. Rastogi left for the office, I could catch him. He was surprised to see me there instead of at the office and asked with concern, "Gupta Sahib! How come you are here? What happened? Hope all is well?"

I said, "Rastogi Ji! There is some problem today and I can not attend the office as my wife Leela is not well."

Rastogi Ji understood and nodded his head.

He as well as everyone at the office knew about my good connections with Kirstein Sahib.

He replied kindly, "Yes, of course! So you want me to inform Sahib that you are on leave today?"

I said, "Yes, my friend. Leela is in bad health."

Rastogi Ji agreed without hesitation, "Do not worry. Take care of your wife. I will convey your message to him."

Thanking him and feeling relieved, I rushed back home, to take care of Leela.

In the meanwhile, Dr. Acharya Ji, Railways' authorised doctor, was already at my house carrying out Leela's check- up.

The Doctor had found her pulse running slower than normal. He also mentioned that since she looked pale and weak, she should be hospitalised at least for a day.

I wondered, what was happening today? Why were things going against the plans?

Today I was to meet Bagga, after a long time, and was looking forward to it – counting every minute!

Neverthless, it was mandatory that we followed Doctor's instructions.

Without further delay, Leela was taken in the Doctor's tonga to the King George Memorial Hospital at Chowk and Leela was admitted in the general ward by 3 p.m.

Fortunately, Dr. Chaudhury Ji, the Chief gynaecologist in charge was also Leela's consulting gynaecologist.

He checked her and said, "It is good that you have brought her here. She needs to take complete rest, since she is very anaemic. Make sure that you look after her well, and give her healthy and nourishing food. This concerns two lives, and we want the baby to be healthy. Besides, the expectant mother must have enough

strength for a normal delivery. It is very important that sheshould not do any strenuous work. She can not bear the physical stressof any kind."

Mataji, person with knowledge about the planets and the astrological calendars, was talking to Leela's mother, "Bahenji, (sister) isn't it Amavasya (no moon night) today? We have to take good care of Leela bahu (daughter-in-law) during such heavy days,' and added further with concern, 'but you need not worry. We are here to take good care of her. I will send some healthy food for her to the hospital."

I was feeling guilty, and practically torn between my duties towards my best friend and Leela's sibling. On second thoughts, it was imperative that I attend to Leela and her baby, our first child. Satish would agree with me, I was sure.

So this was it. I resigned to the fact that I would be staying at the hospital to look after Leela tonight.

I decided to go and meet Lalaji in the evening to convey my decision. Perhaps I should also try to sneak out to reach the Bada Imambara at midnight, but the hospital was very far from the destination, almost on the other side of the city. The mission looked impossible. After giving some thought to it, I dropped the idea of going there myself as well as meeting Lalaji.

Instead, I called Birendra, who was at the back and call, and had readily helped me today. He had grown matured and responsible, with a quiet stance like Banvari.

I said, "Biru! I need your help."

He replied, "Order.. Uncle! I am ready." I was searching for the suitable words.

From where to begin and what to expect from him?

I tried to narrate in short - from the time Satish left home, to meeting him tonight at the Bada Imambara. I explained to him that looking at the situation, it was not possible to meet him any more. He should convey this message to Bagga. Biru was listening intently, and would give a nod in between gesturing that he understood everything.

Much to my surprise, he remained unperturbed, or was he excited to be part of the adventure?

Finally, he said, "Do not worry Uncle! I shall go there tonight as your messenger."

I felt foolish to see his enthusiasm. While I was finding excuses to avoid meeting Satish at night, this boy was all set to take a huge risk. Was I pushing him?

A scary thought crossed my mind. What if he joins Satish's group? No, that should not happen!

Unaware of anything, Leela was sleeping peacefully. She looked relaxed and out of trouble after medication and rest.

I was much relieved. It was necessary to admit her at the hospital after all. With a relaxed mind, I tried to sleep, on the bedding that Biru had got from home.

It was early morning when I heard some footsteps in the corridor. It had to be Birendra. Yes, he was back.

Birendra entered the hospital ward quietly, and sat down next to me. He was breathless. I gave him some water to drink. Birendra spoke in a hushed tone, "I met Uncle Bagga! I met all of them!"

I was surprised and alerted "Who?" and added to clarify, "Who were the people you met other than Bagga?"

Birendra's voice was trembling with eagerness. "Uncle was there and two more persons, one of whom looked like a leader." That interested me. I sat upright and asked, "Tell me everything."

At that instant Leela woke up with a start. She exclaimed, "Oh Biru! How come you are here at this hour? What happened?"

Before Biru could reply her, I cut short the conversation, "He is here to give a few medicines since the shop was closed downstairs. You don't worry and sleep peacefully."

Without pursuing the conversation any further, I signalled Biru to go downstairs where visitors of the patients slept. It was futile for Biru to return home at this hour, lest questions would be asked. Next morning, Gupta Uncle, Leela's father came with tea and food for us, and to relieve me to attend the office.

Since I could not meet Bagga as per the plans, or know more about him from Biru, I was very curious to know more about the meeting and Bagga's group mates.

Next day was Sunday. In the evening Leela would be discharged. So I went to the hospital to bring her home.

We reached home safely in an hour by a tonga which was generously arranged by Kirstein Sahib.

Everyone at home took good care to make sure that Leela did not take extra strain.

We had already engaged a domestic helper, from the railway staff, who would now do all the household chores and help Leela with cooking and other needs. I had also requested Birendra to come and stay with us.

Birendra was now eligible for the college studies after clearing Matriculation exams last year, but he had not so far enrolled himself for the college admission and I wanted to make sure that he did.

Next week, I was lying on my bed at night, after dinner, enjoying cool, natural breeze of the summers.

After a few moments Birendra ate his meals and came out.

I was delighted to see him. In fact, I was thinking about him only.

"Come, Biru! Did you have dinner?" I asked. He replied, "Yes, Uncle", and sat on the floor in front of me.

I said, "Biru, I am so happy that you are staying with us."

Biru happily agreed. I knew he was very fond of Leela and me. He said, "I am privileged."

I asked casually, "So, what are your study plans? Have you decided anything?"

He looked down, and evaded the reply. I understood, it was not the right time to raise this issue.

I tried to discontinue the topic, "There is no hurry. We can talk about it later."

He seemed to gather some courage and replied finally, "Uncle! I am thinking differently."

I clarified, 'Of course, I would not mind if you want to go to a bigger city like Delhi for your college studies.'

Birendra said softly, "It is not that. I was thinking about Uncle Satish."

I offered a tempting option, "Please do evaluate the possibilities of studying science, and become a doctor or an engineer? I shall finance your studies."

The promise made to Birendra was not easy to fulfil though. I was managing the household with my Railways salary with difficulty as the time passed.

Gupta Uncle had grown old suddenly. He had reached the retirement age, and however hard their family tried to save money, it was difficult for them to survive within the limited resources, with Banvari and Satish not around. Besides, due to the big expenses which were incurred in our marriage.

Biru's reply was abrupt. I knew it was coming. "Uncle!... I do not want to study further."

I sat up with a start.

I had yet to gather the information about his meeting with Satish. Was this reply the result of that or anything else?

I observed that Biru's composure was in complete contrast to my feeling of agitation.

He was quite composed.

He stood up and spoke, "Uncle! I want to work for my country. I am inspired by Panditji, Shachin da and the others. I want to become like them."

I slowly realised that he was talking about the meeting with Satish and his groupmates.

I had heard these names often from Lalaji, but had never imagined that they would come all the way to my town, Lucknow, and I would miss out on meeting them.

Bagga had brought them to meet me! But why?

I must know more. I tried to act ignorant. 'Oh you mean the meeting with Bagga. That is so interesting! So these were the two persons with Satish. And how is Satish, my friend?'

Biru was excited at the mention of their names, "Uncle! You should see how strong they are! We must help them in this cause."

To discourage Birendra, I said sarcastically, "So they have instigated you to join their party of revolutionaries?"

If Birendra was annoyed, he did not show it.

He continued quietly, "Uncle, they will never instigate anyone to join them. They are playing with their own lives only."

I couln't allow this to happen again in my house, as a responsible officer of the Indian Railways.

Exasperated, I almost shouted, 'Biru! What shall I answer to your grandparents?'

"You need not worry Uncle! I shall write to them when I leave the house. There is no need to announce it now, please. And I shall not leave Lucknow."

It was difficult to find out what was going on in his mind. Was he another Satish in the making? It was futile asking him anything further. This was my last try.

I went near Birendra and putting my arm around his shoulders, I said, "Okay Biru! Though I do not agree with this, let us not decide in haste, but you very well know what happened with both your uncles. I am sure you do not want to follow their dangerous path."

Birendra seemed lost. "No one has lived fully who has not fought for his motherland's freedom, Uncle Bagga." then abruptly added, "I told him about Aunty Leela's health. He understood."

In almost a whisper, he added, 'Uncle wanted you to meet his group members. They might come to Lucknow again maybe after a month or two.'

Thank God! It was a kind of relief that I could not meet Bagga and his groupmates the last time.

And yet Bagga wanted to meet me? What can be the reason? Did he want a favour from me? My mind bombarded a series of questions. I almost shouted, "No, No!" Then hastily added, "Yes, I shall meet him."

I was anticipating Biru to provide some clue, or throw light on their purpose to meet me, and what he said shocked me further.

'You need not worry, Uncle. They will contact you when everything is cleared.'

For a moment, my faithful services to the British Government, appeared to be going down the drain.

I felt threatened. Didn't I always make clear that I was not interested in participating in the fight against the British Raj? I was not going to throw away my goodwill just like that.

Birendra interrupted my thoughts. "Okay Uncle! I take your leave. I have some work now." And he left like a lightening, leaving me jaw-dropped with the information.

As the new day began, I gradually forgot about Biru and his decision.

I was busy looking after my wife Leela, so that a healthy, strong child is born to her.

Leela's health was much better now. Her parents were extra careful for their daughter too. She was their only source of happiness. And obviously, they were doting on me for almost everything.

At the appropriate time, Leela gave birth to a healthy little bundle of joy, a beautiful baby girl. She was like a princess to all of us, bringing happiness to everyone in the family.

Both my parents and Leela's parents were overjoyed!

In spite of everything, I wanted Satish to be around to share the good news. How happy he and Banvari would be to learn this news!

I purchased a lot of sweets and went to the office. Kirstein Sahib was his same charming self like always and gracefully accepted the sweets. I also distributed it among my collegues.

Kirstein Sahib appeared to be in a relaxed mood that day, and started asking about my family, and my little daughter.

In an effervescent mood, I blurted out information which was not necessary, and mentioned Satish and Banvari absent-mindedly.

Later try as much as I would, I could not recall exactly what I had told my boss about my best friend.

It could have been something like "I have a friend who is both maternal and paternal Uncle to my child, and I am waiting to meet him."

Looking back on this incident, I realised that his expressions flickered for a moment.

Instead of asking anything further, Kirstein Sahib smiled and said, "That is wonderful! What is your friend's name and where is he working?"

His words brought me back to the senses with a jolt.

I was at my defensive best, "Sir, He is working in Delhi. After completion of his graduation, he has shifted to Delhi for a business. But he shall soon be here."

Kirstein Sahib nodded and did not ask anything further.

After the usual office work, I reached Lalaji's shop and gave him the good news.

Lalaji congratulated me. He asked, 'What do you plan to name your daughter?'

I had not thought about it as yet.

I said, 'Since it is Mother Goddess who has entered my house, I will name her Laxmi!'

Lalaji seemed delighted to hear this. With a pleasant feeling, I left him to return home.

Our daughter's name was selected by Leela and me and was appreciated by all the elders in the family.

Laxmi was an active child, and a source of happiness and entertainment for the whole family.

Time flew in her presence and she started growing into a lovely little girl doted on by everyone.

At the office, with the work mounting up, conversation I had with Biru was out of my mind. Besides, it was not possible for me to keep a constant vigil on him or ask questions.

Eventually, within a few days the situation revealed itself to me.

Much to my surprise, Birendra was seeking an opportunity to talk to me. He came to me on a Sunday.

"Yes, Biru?" I looked at him suspiciously. "Some time ago I met Uncle Bagga."

This was like going through the painful memories again.

"How is Satish?" My voice trembled, I could not deceive my feelings and sank in the chair.

"Uncle, you will be proud when you know about the work he and his groupmates are doing!"

Utter silence from me made Biru divert the topic.

"Uncle Satish was asking about you and Aunty Leela and..."

This meant that something important was coming up. I looked at him with concern.

'Did he? What did he say?'

"He is coming to Lucknow next week. He wants to meet you."

I needed time to absorb the news and give it a thought. It was not easy to reply immediately.

At that instant, Leela came into the room holding Laxmi, who was a toddler now, and said, "Please look after her. I have to finish a few chores in the kitchen."

This left no room for further talk with Biru. A lot remained unsaid. I was facing the reality now. Did I really want to meet Satish? How safe that would be? The hands of the British Emperor and his men were too long. There was an air of deep suspicion all over.

What if the police was following them?

My job at the Indian Railways had earned me a good reputation and a steady income with two successive promotions. I had started earning enough to feed the two families. All this would be at stake and was not affordable at any cost.

I hoped Biru, Satish and Banvari understood and respected this important aspect to life sometimes.

I reached my office, and tried to put aside the thoughts of Biru and Satish, but it was all in vain.

This conversation had left me disturbed and agitated.

After Bagga had left the house, it was a usual practice with him to visit the city on the Amavasya (no moon) day.

The next Amavasya was after a few days. In all probability, Bagga would be here on that day. My fears turned out to be justified.

In the last week of July, Biru was waiting for me when I reached home from the office. "Uncle, tomorrow evening you will haveto come with me."

I could sense the purpose. With some effort, I replied, 'I am not sure Biru.'

"Uncle, this is very important. Uncle Satish has conveyed that he would be at the Bada Immambara after mignight."

Despite my unwillingness, I decided to meet my old friend Bagga this time. I wanted to know about his life - how did he survive and what kind of life did he lead?

My old self, Bagga's best friend Mukund- decided to reach home early that day.

Being a senior officer now, there were very few restrictions on my working hours. Besides, my inherent self-discipline had always prevented me from taking any liberties otherwise.

Keeping in mind my meeting with Bagga, I left the office early at around 5.30 p.m. I instructed my Junior Officer, Ramnarayan Tiwari Ji accordingly.

"I have to go home a little early. Is there any urgent work to be completed today?"

"No Saheb, just one thing, guard Jagmohan was seeking your permission to grant him leave from the next month."

"Okay, what route is he working on?"

"Sir, between Shahjahanpur and Lucknow."

"Theek hai. Tell him to come and meet me tomorrow."

In one year of my association with Kirstein Sahib, I had earned a great trust from him. Admittedly, it was his good heartedness, that he considered me to be worthy of becoming his successor.

The Indian Railways company had recently gifted me a bicycle after my last promotion. This was their gesture to appreciate the work of a few officers, and I was one of them. I considered myself really fortunate about it. This made my commuting to the office much easier.

The British administration had certainly changed India's picture by their good planning and modernisation and it was never enough to thank them for the technology and discipline that they had brought about in our country.

My faithfulness towards the Raj was deep and unshakeable especially after becoming an Indian Railways employee. It was a proud moment for me that I was in the good books of all the Government officers including the Police Department of Lucknow.

Thanks to Kirstein Sahib, I was often invited to their parties, and sometimes to their confidential meetings.

I was never doubted or questioned by the Police in Lucknow, though my family was not free from the suspicion, for the obvious reasons of course.

It was ironical that I had to restrict this opinion to myself, Leela being Bagga and Banvari's sister, and Biru - who was now staying with us would never agree with me.

Whenever, I came across a police constable or a CID official, they would talk to me in a friendly way, and would make it a point to mention about Banvari and Satish, emphasising that they were under constant suspicion of the British Police, and their alleged connections with the revolutionary groups.

On the other hand, if I happen to meet Bagga today, I would be putting all my goodwill at a stake.

"No, no, I shall refrain from meeting Satish," I kept telling myself. Why would Satish want to contact me?

Should I ask Biru the purpose of meeting? After much brain storming on this issue, I decided to ask Biru clearly about what was going on.

Little Laxmi came running to me when I returned from the office, but I could not express my joy or be playful with her today. Instead, I went straight into my room, and lay down to relax.

As the evening set in, Birendra returned home. He seemed disturbed.

I was curious. “Biru, is everything okay?”

“Yes, Uncle - No, Uncle I am fine.” This was certainly not how Biru would reply. Something was wrong somewhere.

Within a few minutes, he rushed out of the house again. This was not normal.

It was necessary to be strict with him for his safety and well being. I should ask him a few questions directly.

Biru finally returned home around 10:00 pm. My inquisitiveness and worry had not allowed me to sleep.

Birendra went to the backyard to wash himself, I followed him. “Biru, what is the matter?”

“Woh…”

“Don’t be afraid. Tell me the truth.”

Before Biru could disclose anything, there was a sharp knock at the door.

I had to quickly open the door, only to find a policeman standing at the door. This was shocking but it also made sense now.

Perhaps Biru was being followed by the Police.

"Aayie, aayie, Sinha Saheb! Yahan kaise aana hua?" (Welcome, Sinha Saheb! What brings you here?) I tried to put on a friendly tone.

"Namaste Pandey Ji! Yeh aapka ghar hai kya? Hamne ek shakmand vyakti ko yaha aate hue dekha hai." (Namaste Pandeji! We saw one suspect entering this house.)

"Saheb, it is not possible. Ye to hamara bhanja (sister's son) Birendra hai." (He is my nephew Birendra).

"Biru, jara bahar aao." (Biru, please come outside).

I called Biru. He took some time to come out, and greeted the police constable. "Beta, tum vahan nadi ke kinare gaye the kya?" (Son, did you go to the river bank?)

"Mai tau paas se guzar raha tha chachaji." (Uncle, I was just passing by.)

I intervened. "Sinha Saheb, I can gurantee for him. He will notdo anything that is against the Government."

Sinha Saheb was a strict Police Officer, like all the British policemen.

"Theek hai Pandeji, aap kahete ho tau is baar mai jane deta hu. (Okay Panditji. I shall let him go this time if you say so.) I do not want any nonsense happening in Lucknow. Already the revolutionaries have started looting villages and other places. They are making bombs in the houses and schools. We have to be strict with every person."

He looked at me and added, "When you already have your brother-in-laws as the suspects, do take care Pandey Ji, and always be in good books of the Raj, to be safe and happy."

Trembling from inside, I tried to calm him down. "Ye galti kaise ho sakti hai Sinha Saheb? (Sinha Sir, how can I commit such a mistake?) If I happen to meet a revolutionary tomorrow, I myself shall bring him to the police station."

He nodded with a smile and departed.

After a few minutes, when it was certain that Sinha Saheb was away from the vicinity,

Biru blurted out, "That is exactly what Uncle Bagga wants you to do tomorrow!"

I was angry at his audacity. "Biru, I have decided. No meetings with the freedom fighters. And I shall also not allow you to meet with them, if that is what you have been doing. The Police is already keeping a track of your movements."

"Okay", Biru abruptly ended the conversation, and went out of the room.

With a disturbing thought that the things were not happening right, I entered the room where Leela was asleep. On second thoughts, I apprehended that she had heard our conversation.

There was no question of going to meet Bagga tonight. Sinha Saheb had completely sealed all possibilities.

Next day, I reached office at the usual time, and again got too busy with the work, to hardly remember yesterday's events.

At around 4 pm, my assistant Tiwari Ji came to me. "Saheb, Jagmohan is here. Shall I send him to you?"

"Okay send him in."

Jagmohan was an old man, nearing his retirement, and was known for his sincere services to the Indian Railways. He was one of the oldest employees here, who had provided more than 40 years of services to the Company. In all the probability, he would earn the Best Employee's award in the Guards' category soon, was what everyone assumed. I had always liked him.

"Come in Jagmohan! How are you?"

"Namaste Saheb! Aap ke saath reh kar khush hoon" (Salutes Sir! I am happy to be with you!) He spread happy vibes.

"Kaho (speak)."

"Saheb, I want three days' leave from work."

"You already took leave last month for a week. Why again? Hope all is well?"

"Ji Saheb, that was to decide the wedding date of my grand-daughter. And now we all shall visit her in-laws' place."

"So you will be enjoying the hospitality of your samdhis (in-laws of son or daughter)."

"Saheb, in fact we have to go and give them some money and ornaments (dowry token) before they change their mind."

This conversation reminded me of the painful memories of Leela's deceased sisters, and so many other girls in our society. I strongly believed that something should be done to change this age-old marriage system of extorting money from the bride's family. Maybe some changes can be brought about in the social systems with the help of the British Government, who will understand the pathetic rituals prevalent in the Indian society, and will try to demolish them.

I took a deep breath. "Jagmohan! I wish I could help you in some way, since you have mortgaged your land for this. However, I shall not deny you the leave. By the way, where have you to go?"

"Kakori, Saheb. It's not very far."

"Okay, give your leave application and I shall sign it."

"Thank you Saheb." Jagmohan folded his hands thankfully. "When do you plan to return?"

"Saheb, I shall try to be back by the 5th of August." It was indisputable to doubt Jagmohan's promise. He usually returned a day prior to his leave getting over, but not later.

I asked Tiwari Ji, "Who will take charge of the shift in place of Jagmohan?"

He replied, "There is one new recruit, ShivDayal. He is a young boy, who is ready to work for long hours. Looks promising for the job."

I sanctioned Jagmohan's leave, keeping in mind that Tiwari Ji had the replacement ready. He had a knack for selecting new recruits.

"Jagmohan, before you go on leave, teach ShivDayal your system of working, and explain to him all the precautions and especially the danger signals. We do not want any accidents, now that Indian Railways is doing so well in the British Raj."

Jagmohan folded his hands. "Yes, Saheb. Do not worry, that is my duty, and I shall put in my best. ShivDayal is son of my distant cousin."

Besides he has some work experience in the Railways as well, so he will learn the task quickly. You will have no reason to complain.

This sorted out, I left the office, and reached home in some time.

The last few days' happenings had been giving me a jittery feeling. Neither did I want to face it, nor wanted to ignore Sinha's warning. What made me so restless? I felt as if I was playing the game of tug of war all the time, outside as well as within myself.

Should I confide in Leela? Would she be able to understand all the notorious and anti-British activities of her brothers and the nephew? I was not sure.

As I reached home, little Laxmi was waiting for me to take her out. Today, I did not want to disappoint her. In fact, I looked forward to it as well.

After having tea, I took her out for a small walk and soon forgot about all my uneasiness.

By the time I returned, the dinner was ready to be served.

Due to heavy work load at the office, I had carried some files home and had to complete the pending office work at night.

The elaborate calculations were tedious and took longer time than expected. As a result, I was working till late night for the reports to be sent to Delhi the next day.

The next morning was a bright, sunny day. It had rained the previous night, and I felt as if the rain had washed away my restlessness with it.

It was the first week of August, and I was already looking forward to Sunday's holiday.

In a happy state of mind, I left early for the office, since I had to send the reports urgently to Delhi.

As anticipated, around the lunch time, I received a telegram from the Delhi Head Office, requesting to send the detailed calculations as per the new budget, but to my utter shock, I realised that, in haste I had left the files at home.

The Railway office owned its own tonga, which I decided to use for today's emergency.

I hurriedly got in the tonga, and told the tongaman to quickly take me to my home. Very quickly he covered the distance, and soon I reached near to my home.

I was about to reach home, when I was thunderstruck to see something unexpected. Someone resembling Leela was standing at Lalaji's paan shop. No. no.., I looked again! This must be my mistake.

I tried to look at her intently and closely. She was a woman with a thin and delicate body structure very similar to Leela's, but by now she had covered her head with the pallu (end of saree) of her saree. Interestingly, in our liberal household, Leela was allowed to keep her head open, so in all probability, she can not be Leela.

However hard I tried, I could not confirm whether it was Leela or someone else. I saw this woman for only a fraction of a minute, and it was not possible to stop the tonga due to urgency of the situation.

Then the tonga took a turn around the bend in the road and the shop vanished from my eyes in no time.

As soon as I reached home, I anxiously started looking for Leela and called aloud, 'Leela! Leela!'

Mataji opened the door slowly. She had become so frail now. 'What is it bete? (son) Leela will come back soon. She has gone to fetch some vegetables.'

I was aghast not to find Leela at home. Was she then at the Lalaji's shop? Although, I had no time to spy on my dear wife at this moment. The Delhi Office was waiting for a report from me, which had to be sent at the earliest, and I must hurry up.

I took the files from the table and hastily returned to the office.

On my way back, I was very anxious to discover more about the woman at the Lalaji's shop, and rule out the possibility of Leela's presence there, but unfortunately no one was to be seen now.

It would be stupid to wait there and search for her or ask Lalaji. By the time I reached office, it was nearing lunch time.

I made sure to send the reports as quickly as possible to the Head Office, to fulfil my responsibility.

Once the dispatching was over, I heaved a sigh of relief.

Nerverthless, there was no relief to my ever-questioning mind. I had to find out what was going on at home front. What if my wife in reality was the woman at Lalaji's shop? A mere thought of it was like opening the Pandora's box.

I anxiously waited for the office to be over, and rushed home immediately. It was a great relief to find Leela playing innocently with our sweet daughter Laxmi, in the front courtyard.

After looking at her pleasant demeanour I felt very stupid for judging her wrongly. "Of course, she could never be helping her brothers or working against the Raj." I told myself and was completely convinced and feeling utterly relieved.

Once I got over the doubt, all the concern associated with Bagga, Biru and his group of revolutionaries disappeared from my mind. I prayed to God that when my reports reach Delhi, I would be designated as one of the most competent and sincere employees of the Indian Railways.

What a myth were my thoughts!

Let me admit that I was wrong in underestimating Leela's strength and her devotion towards the freedom fight and that by the patriotic men and women of India. Unfortunately, it was too late by the time I learnt about it.

The events that followed the next week were going to be etched in the history of India's Freedom Struggle indelibly, with its repercussions affecting everyone in our family fully and tragically.

❑

6

The Kakori Train Robbery

(A) The Conclusion

Leelavati Narrates

What happened on the 9th August, 1925?

Alas! The world knows only one-sided story, but no one knows the cost that our family had to pay due to that incident- the famous 'Kakori Robbery' which was an important turning point in the history of India's Freedom Struggle.

My husband Mukund Ji, in spite of being Bagga Bhaiya's best friend, never supported him or Banvari Bhaiya. He disagreed with them all along, their ideology and their fight against the British Raj.

Fortunately, Mukund Ji never came to know that I was connected with my brothers and Biru in this fight since the beginning. If he had known it, things might have been different. Perhaps he would never have married me, or he himself would have joined hands with us. Or perhaps not. Ironically, the end was the same for everyone.

Biru had been in touch with the freedom fighters since long, thus continuing to be a reliable messenger for me, helping in sending and receiving messages from both my brothers.

I was now advised not to act as a post box by the group. There was a fear of being caught by the Police, especially after Banvari Bhaiya was imprisoned again.

The group had sent an alert message via Biru that our family was under constant observation, and a small mistake would land me in the hot waters, which subsequently would mean a very deep trouble for all of them and Mukund Ji.

The terror of Rai Bahadur Chatterjee and the British Police, always loomed large on us, both of whom kept finding excuses to visit our house either to meet my parents and to judge the situation or to see if any suspicious development was there.

Since the last few months, Biru used to keep me updated about robbery of the money from the rich zamindaars (landlords) and the wealthy villagers, carried out by Bagga Bhaiya's group. They said that the thefts were executed ethically, without harming any one. I was not convinced though and had some doubts and fears of my own.

The money so extracted, which was called FC (Financial Contribution) was accumulated for sustaining the group mates, buying weapons, and other miscellaneous expenses. In fact, whatever money or ornaments they looted, were often sent to me, or dropped at our house by some unkown people during the odd hours at night.

Keeping awake at night was very normal for me. I had to get up for feeding little Laxmi or when she needed some care during the odd hours.

It was during the last week of July that I heard Biru talking to Mukund Ji. It surprised me greatly that he was trying to involve Mukund Ji and requesting him to meet Bagga Bhaiya's groupmates. This was a futile hope.

Mukund Ji would never support the revolutionaries, a fact which I knew very well.

As anticipated, on Biru's insistance to meet Bagga Bhaiya, Mukund Ji sounded very offended and refused point blank to meet or extend help of any kind.

The next morning after Mukund Ji left for the office, I asked Biru, "Why are you trying to involve him, when he is so committed to the Raj?"

Biru replied, "Mausi, baat hi kuch aisi hai." (Aunty, the matter is such.)

It was a complete secret, but Biru shared it with me. As per the information, an unexpected plan was taking shape - Bagga Bhaiya's group had decided to rob a train carrying treasury.

I was really scared to hear this. This was like challenging the British Police and the Government face to face. It was suicidal ....walking into the death trap knowingly.

I told Biru in exasperation, "This is like playing with the fire. No one will survive if anything goes wrong."

Ironically, Biru agreed too. "Mausi, sabhi ye baat jante hai. (Aunty, all know about this.) That is why we need Uncle Mukund's help. We shall try to make the whole incident appear as if it was the Railways Department's fault."

This sounded ridiculous and made me very upset. I could never even in my dreams imagine Mukund Ji supporting the freedom fighters.

During my conversation with Biru, Laxmi had been crying for long with hunger, but I could not realise it till Mataji came and drew my attention to it.

Comprehending my agitation, Biru came up with some more information to pacify me.

"Aunty, in this conspiracy, two very reliable persons are planted by our group on the route who will help us. Jagmohan Chacha and Ravindra Mohan (Shiv Dayal). If anything goes wrong, they would protect us, and the whole plan will be covered up."

I was not aware of what Bagga Bhaiya was expecting from Mukund Ji, but it was my fear that a weak and incomplete link remained unaddressed.

Deep within my heart, I felt clueless and afraid. What if they were caught? What if the police started firing on the spot?

As per Biru's information, this plan was likely to be implemented during the first week of August. As soon as money from the railway treasury was collected, one of their group members would hand it over to me, which I was to deposit with Lalaji Paanwala on the same day, and if it got late, then by the next morning.

The excitement was growing, but Biru and I had to appear calm at home, carrying on the routine chores normally. We also had to be very careful about our own whereabouts during these days to create a convincing proof. Biru assured me and told me not to worry too much.

It was already the 7th of August, since the plan was in its final stages, I thought of asking Lalaji about a signal for going ahead.

I made an excuse for fetching some vegetables, requesting Mataaji to take care of Laxmi, I rushed out to meet Lalaji.

It was around noon. Nobody else was at home, and Mukund Ji was at the office. Biru was also not home since last two days, busy preparing for the final co-ordination with the group.

I reached Lalaji's shop in 15 minutes. He welcomed me happily and shared some latest information on the big game plan.

"Aao Bitiya! Mai tumhe sandesha bhejnewala hi tha. (Welcome daughter! I was about to send you a message!) You come to pick up the next paan on the 8th, that is tomorrow."

He added, "It is Saturday, is it a holiday at home?"

I replied, "No, no, Chachaji, we work on Saturdays, but not on Sundays. Hence, I can not come on Sunday, but will be there on Monday morning."

"I understand." He had hardly completed his sentence, when we saw a tonga approaching towards the shop. There were very few tongas in Lucknow, so that it was very unusual to find one at this hour and that too in this area.

Suddenly, Lalaji sounded an alert warning, "Cover your head, child."

It did not take me long to realise that the person sitting in the tonga could be my husband, since he had the prerogative to use it for the emergency purposes related to the Railway Office.

Without waiting for a second, I covered my head, and started acting like a woman from a different community, where the women stretch hands while talking. I began acting like a dumb and lost person, who was asking for the directions at Lalaji's shop.

I recollected that yesterday night Mukund Ji was working till late, and had forgotton the files at home, while leaving for the office in the morning.

Lalaji's instant idea saved me from a blunder. Without wasting any time, I left the shop and took the different road to my house. I stopped at the sabji-mandi lest I forget to buy some vegetables, picked up a few randomly and reached home as early as I could.

However, I could only reach home in twenty minutes, when I saw that Mataji was waiting for me anxiously.

"Where were you, Leela? Mukund had come home, to fetch some files. Hope he does not keep forgetting things often under so much workload. I wish you were there."

I mumbled, "Yes, Maaji" without any discussion and took charge of Laxmi, and got busy with the household.

Though, Mukund Ji was not of suspicous nature, I wanted to make doubly sure, and changed the saree before he was home, to rule out any doubts.

In the evening, when Mukund Ji returned from the office, I had got Laxmi ready to be taken out for a stroll. I could sense that he wanted to ask me something, or was in a dilemma, but Laxmi's excitement to go out, pursuaded him to forget about the afternoon episode. Thanking Lalaji's spontaneity and my stars, I decided never to make such a mistake again. It could have ruined my life.

The next morning Biru came home. He looked tired and exhausted. 'Aunty, give me something to eat. I have been running around so much. I am exhausted and starving.'

"Yes, Biru."

At that moment Mukund Ji came in the kitchen to say that he was leaving.

"What keeps you so busy, Biru? Kabhi ghar pe bhi dikha karo." (Stay at home sometimes).

"Uncle, I am at home all the time. Ask Mausi!"

I tried to divert the discussion, and made sure that Mukund Ji left home in a quiet frame of mind.

As soon as he was gone, I hurriedly gave some food to Biru. After he finished eating, I narrated to him what had happened the previous day, and that the 8th August was fixed as the final date.

"Yes, I know it. I was with two of them only. They have already arrived here."

I looked at Biru, who in spite of being exhausted looked happy and satisfied. I could sense a spark of confidence in him now. Then all of a sudden, I was reminded of Bagga Bhaiya and Banvari Bhaiya.

"What are we supposed to do Biru?"

"Nothing much.... just help anyone who comes home tired, and offer food and shelter. Perhaps Uncle Bagga might come here with one more groupmate."

8th August arrived. It was the usual Saturday morning. Today, Mukund Ji would return early from the office.

I was waiting eagerly for the evening and for Biru, who was away since yesterday, to come home and give the much expected happy message. 'All clear!'

The things were not very smooth for me though. Laxmi was unwell since last two days. The medicines had been given by the Railways' authorised Doctor, yet she was not recovering as fast as expected ... and continued to be cranky.

However, my mind was wandering somewhere else. I was peeping out of the house at short intervals till the darkness turned the evening into night.

Mukund Ji seemed to have sensed that I was lost somewhere and was concerned. He asked, "Leela, are you okay? Do not worry so much about Laxmi. She will be fine. There are no ghosts lurking outside our house to trouble you." I smiled lamely to look comforted.

Finally, Laxmi slept, and I dozed off along with her as well.

I do not know how long I slept, but when I woke up, it was early morning. I checked the old wall clock, a marriage gift by my relatives, which indicated it was around 4 am.

"Oh! I missed the follow up. I hope the mission was successful. Why had Biru not returned? What must have happened? Hope all went well and all are safe….."

There was a flood of thoughts that took charge of me. I was eagerly waiting to hear from Biru about the final action that took place in Kakori and what was the outcome.

It was already Sunday, 9th August today. Obviously, Mukund Ji was going to be at home the whole day. It would be difficult to talk to Biru in his presence.

I decided to visit my parents to play safe without drawing any attention. Hoping that when Biru returned home and would come to know about my visit to parents' house, he would follow me and we could talk at length there.

As the morning was unfolding, I announced that I was planning to visit my parents, since I had not met them for long.

Everyone was surprised, but no one prevented me from going there.

"Leela, Laxmi is still recovering from her illness, and do you want to expose her to such weather? It might rain anytime." Mukund Ji tried to convince me that I should postpone it by a day or two. Besides, it was a Sunday.

"No, I think I will manage with Laxmi."

By the time I had finished cooking and the routine chores, it was nearly afternoon.

Seeing my insistence for going, Mukund Ji called the peon from his office, who often worked as a domestic helper as well, and called the office tonga for me.

I was getting frustrated and impatient with the passing of every minute. After some time, the tongawala arrived, and I went to meet my parents.

When I passed by Lalaji's shop, I wanted to jump from the tonga, and ask him about the plan's success but I had to control myself. It was necessary for me to keep quiet and appear normal at the moment.

I reached my parents' home in half an hour. Seeing the door of the house already open, my heart throbbed hard. Biru was standing there.

"Biru..!" What was he doing here at this hour? I was numb with anxiety.

He signalled me to keep quiet and took me to the backyard.

"Biru, sab khairiyat? (Biru, All well?) What happened to the great plan?"

Biru sounded sad. "Thoda sa fark ho gaya. Train chhoot gayi." ('There was a lapse. They missed the train.')

I was thunderstruck. "Ab kya hoga? (What will happen now?)

Hope the plan is still on and not dropped."

"Yes, it will be executed today! But how will they manage?"

> *"That is the hitch. Now it is impossible to get help from Jagmohan Chacha and Shiv Dayal but we shall still go ahead with it come what may."*
>
> *I was devastated and worried that in spite of so much planning, risks taken and the group of Bagga Bhaiya staking their lives, would the plan fail?*

Mataji came and affectionately took Laxmi away to the kitchen.

I did not have anything further to ask Biru, except that we had to wait again for tonight's rendezvous.

Biru explained to me in short that it would be the same as yesterday, so I need not worry and left immediately. The change in the action plan made me very nervous and I started shaking with fear. This was not a good sign.

"What if..." scary thoughts were constantly hammering my mind.

A nagging restlessness took over me and I returned home after a short stay at my parents' house.

Mukund Ji and Mataji were relieved to see me return so soon.

The remaining day passed in a holiday mood for everyone, except for me. This was obvious after receiving the disasterous morning news.

Laxmi was recovering well from her illness, and had started returning to her normal food intake and playfulness, which was a big relief.

Mukund Ji went to visit one of his Railways Office friends in the evening.

Nothing worth mentioning happened during the whole day. Of course, nothing was to happen apparently. Laxmi went to sleep early that night and so did everyone eventually after a quick dinner.

The silence of the night was intolerable today. After every five minutes, I heard a few imaginative sounds, and continued to wait as if someone was going to emerge from the window! Alas! Nothing happened.

I didn't realise when I slept off in the excitement of the situation. It was just before the dawn that I heard the sound of very soft footsteps outside.

I woke up with a start, and came out very quietly in the backyard.

There was a little fence, made up of some plants and shrubs, which separated other houses from ours. It was through this fence that Bagga Bhaiya or his team-mates used to come and meet me on some occasions.

"Leela....." I heard someone calling and turned around to see, but could not find anyone. I wondered if it was my imagination. In a moment a silhouette emerged from the darkness. It was none other than Bagga Bhaiya himself who had come to meet me.

"Is it you Bhaiya?'

He was panting, as if he had done a lot of running, but the excitement of accomplishing a mammoth task was so evident in the atmosphere. I couldn't say anything more. The tears choked my voice.

Bagga Bhaiya came forward and hugged me. "Muniya! Kam ho gaya! (Muniya! Plan is successful!)

I was overjoyed to hear these long-awaited words! So at last my brave brother and his team could beat the King!

I stood speechless for a few moments. Then coming back to life, rushed to the kitchen and brought food for him, which I had kept aside in anticipation and served to him quickly.

I noticed that there was one more person with him, who came out from the darkness, so I gave him something to eat as well.

> *"Both of us will sleep here in the backyard. You will not be asked to take care of anything today. This is a big amount of responsibility. You could be in trouble."*

As Bagga Bhaiya explained, I listened to him quietly, nodding as he was talking. I was as excited as him, but it would be stupid to react at this moment, and brought two bed sheets from inside cautiously.

"Muniya, take it away before sunlight, when we are gone. Today we were successful, but unfortunately Roshan Singh has dropped his shawl on the Railway tracks, so we do not know about tomorrow, anything can happen. You take care. God willing, we will meet soon."

I returned to my bed as quietly as possible, in a futile attempt to sleep again. After hardly two hours, when the dawn was setting in, there was the same sound of the footsteps again, and I knew that they were gone. I got up softly to check, and indeed, the backyard was empty, with only the two bed sheets lying in a corner.

I picked up, folded and brought them inside.

Mukund Ji was half awake by then. "Did anyone come here, Leela?"

"No, no one", I lied. "I had a delusion too, but there is no one." and pretended to go back to sleep.

Monday morning began as usual. The newspaper was dropped at the doorstep as usual at this time of morning.

Mukund Ji always enjoyed reading the fresh newspaper. Today as soon as he read the headlines, he could not contain his shock and almost shouted,

"There has been a train loot! That too on the Lucknow route! I will have to rush to the office!"

In no time, Mukund Ji got ready and rushed to the office.

It was at an unimaginable pace with which the Police was following up on this robbery and searching for any proofs or witnesses.

I was worried for Mukund Ji. It was difficult to find out what was happening at the Railway office.

Mukund Ji did not return home in the evening, he was detained there along with all the employees. It was only after two days of the interrogation and the searches, he returned from the office on Wednesday evening.

Waiting for him was like a nightmare to me. On one hand, the train loot was a great success, but at what cost?

It was shocking to see the state Mukund Ji was in, who could not be recognised. This Mukund Ji was a tired, disappointed man.

After eating some food that I served him, he started talking and sounded devastated.

"This train robbery was an alarming crime for the British Government. To confirm the doubt that this shocking act was not done by the ordinary looters, but carried out by the revolutionaries, the claws of the British Police started growing ruthlessly tighter. Much to our misfortune, they have not spared even me. They are suspecting me, Leela! Me? I gave all my life, my friendship, everything away to help the British Government, and now they accuse me of helping the revolutionaries."

I was speechless. This was very painful. I could not see Mukund Ji in such a helpless situation with no fault of his.

The days after that were terrifying with Police entering our house at odd hours for interrogation, for search with a constant vigil.

Within ten days, the Police – advised by Rai Bahadur Chatterjee - confirmed the doubt that the loot was carried out by none other than the revolutionaries, and it could not be possible without the help or support of someone from the Indian Railways itself.

There was a police warrant out in the name of Mukund Ji.

Despite all the pleading, the police constable Sinha did not show any mercy towards my husband, who was imprisoned, along with at least hundred other suspects.

This was shattering for me and our old parents. This was very unfortunate and the least expected happening. In both the houses, parents were crying and feeling helpless, if only Mukund Ji could be bailed out. My father tried all his government connections, but they were completely indifferent and paid no heed to our pleas.

There were policemen and the detectives all the time keeping a watch outside our house.

Whatever goodwill was created by Mukund Ji by toiling so hard for years and extending reverence towards the Government was destroyed by this event. I considered myself guilty and responsible for what happened to Mukund Ji. Perhaps, he knew about my involvement with the revolutionaries, but took it upon himself to keep me safe.

It was futile to expect Bagga Bhaiya to come home, since he was running a great risk to his own life. His presence could land all of us in trouble as well. After about a month, we got the news of Bagga Bhaiya's arrest from Benaras along with few others.

It was an irony that he was imprisoned with Mukund Ji in the same jail for some time.

Mukund Ji, along with few Railway Officers, all the staff members, Jagmohan Chacha and Shiv Dayal as well as those who were on duty on the 9th August were accused of conspiring against the Government. No mercy was shown to any of them.

My old father and father-in-law both attended all the hearings when 'Kakori Conspiracy' case was tried in the court, and left no stone unturned to approach the renowened lawyers. But everything went in vain.

I used to visit Mukund Ji in the prison sometimes. By now we had started running short of money, so we reduced our meetings as travelling to and from the jail meant spending money. Bagga Bhaiya was in the same jail initially, so our family could meet him simultaniousy. Eventually, he was declared to be one of the prime accused, and was sent to another jail with more vigilance and strictness.

The full details of the conspiracy had been thoroughly investigated by the British Government by investing all the resources, informers and links available. After a few months, the judgement was delivered.

As is natural in such testing circumstances, none of our relatives or acquaintances stayed in touch with us, or came to meet us, let aside helping in any way.

The severity of the British was so formidable that everyone was afraid to be seen with the people who had participated in any activity which was a heinous crime according to the British Police.

No one was spared from our family. Bagga Bhaiya was sent to 'Kaala Pani (Cellular Jail),' the colonial jail in the Andaman Nicobar Islands for tough life imprisonment, from where he never returned. According to the rumours that reached us some months later, he tried to run away from the island, but was caught and mercilessly drowned into the poisonous waters with the crocodiles and snakes all around.

Since Bagga Bhaiya was accused of being an integral part of the 'Kakori Conspiracy', Banvari Bhaiya's jail sentence prolonged and he fell ill in the Jail Hospital. Pehaps, he developed tuberculosis, and could hardly survive for two painful years.

We were not permitted to see him as well during his last days.

The misfortune had struck us completely. My innocent husband, Mukund Ji and fifteen other employees from the Railways who worked at the Kakori Railway Station, including the Station Master, guards, etc. were not remissioned. The innocent souls suffered for no fault of theirs. Perhaps, they contributed in the good cause by going through unbearable sufferings.

After the case was closed, one fine day, they were all taken to the Kakori Railway Station. Nothing was disclosed to any of them, or their family members.

However, in the evening their dead bodies were sent to their respective houses.

I was informed by our neighbour that they were hanged on the banyan tree outside the Kakori Railway Station to create terror and set an example to the people.

It was painfully torturous to see both Pitaji and my father- in- law performing the last rites of Mukund Ji. I was struck by guilt and held myself responsible for Mukund Ji's untimely, unfortunate and undeserved sufferings and subsequent painful death besides the loss of his well-earned respect and prestige. He perhaps knew that I was a link in the revolutionary chain, yet he never embarrassed me by asking me or let me fall into the clutches of the inhuman British Police.

I never saw Biru again. I got to know from Lalaji after about six months that he had run away to Singapore, and joined the 'Indian National Army' founded by Netaji Subhash Chandra Bose. Since then, many years have passed, and I do not know whether he is alive or dead in the Independent India.

One of our distant relatives told me that his brother had met Biru when he was being captured during the British rule with the other INA soldiers and was kept in captivity in the Salimgarh Fort in Chandni Chowk. No soldier ever survived and returned alive from the beastly tortures of the British from Salimgarh. Biru too never returned.

Since it was futile to expect any pension from the Indian Railways after the 'Kakori Trials,' I had to start working and earning, by doing some petty household work and cloth-stitching, or whatever work was available to provide for the daily expenses and the important medicines for both

Our parents too did not survive for long, they being completely shattered after loss of their dear sons who were to support them in their old age.

They died within a span of two to three years. The shock of losing all the young boys of both the family gradually led all four of them towards death.

Ultimately, the news of India becoming an independent nation reached me. Some of the relatives of revolutionaries suggested that I should apply for the pension which was given to the families of freedom fighters. I tried to contact the local office at Lucknow, but no one was neither ready to listen to me or ready to help.

It was shocking to see that people who betrayed the nation and the fighters and who had turned into informers passing on the information to the British Government, were felicitated with high posts and good money as reward.

I wonder, if this was the same country for which my brothers, husband and nephew and thousands of other freedom fighters underwent the tyranny of the British and were subjected to humiliations and sacrificed their lives.

In free India, the Government had completely forgotten about sacrifices of the unsung heroes like Satish Bhaiya, Banvari Bhaiya, and Biru, forget about giving any support to their families.

They never even recognised the sincere services and undying loyalties of the hundreds and thousands of Indians who worked industriously for the British Government like Mukund Ji.

Now my sole ray of hope is Laxmi. She has been bequeathed patriotism from her uncles, and studious nature from her father. She studied hard to become the first 'Lady Police Officer' of the Independent India, and has chosen to work at the Lucknow Jail, a place where her father and two uncles had spent their last days.

Yes, she is a strong woman of the new and rising India. Everyday we can see so many young and patriotic girls and boys like her emerging from all the corners of the country. Why not? This is our sacred land which was made fertile by the blood of freedom fighters.

It was certain that the seeds sown in the soil would grow into trees encompassing the whole country with brightness of the New India.

As the bright sun of tomorrow shall rise in the sky, I shall depart from this world to meet my brothers and husband in the world beyond.

The life now appears to be worthless without those with whom I had spent my childhood, knitted the dreams of the free India, participated in a conspiracy against the tyrants in my own way and lost all in the process. Laxmi is an independent girl and I am certain of her success. I can leave peacefully now....with a heartfelt prayer and an advice to the new generation.

(B)The Facts

What actually happened during the Kakori Train Robbery on the 9th August, 1925?

Penned by Ram Prasad Bismil

If we could collect money in good amount, then we could buy enough weapons to fight systematically against the British. Not only that, we could also get machine guns made according to our requirements. But we were not doing good financially at that point of time.

No one was either ready to donate money or to give by way of loan to us.

The situation was getting very desperate, but the last thing I wanted to do was to loot the innocent Indian citizens every time.

I was eager to extract the Government money from somewhere, but nothing was working out.

During one of those days, I had to travel by train, and I was sitting in the boggie next to the Railway Guard's boggie.

When the train reached the next station, the Station Master came with a heavy iron box and put it in the Guard's boggie. Then I heard a 'click' sound, as if something being locked.

I got down to see what it was, I saw that it was a big iron box, I guessed that the iron box must be containing treasury money.

Same procedure followed at the next station as well.

Perhaps the big box was locked tightly with a lock or a chain.

I registered this information mentally, but nothing further could be discovered. After a few days, on another occasion, while visiting Lucknow station, I observed that the coolies were unloading some iron boxes, and it occurred to me that these were perhaps the same ones that I saw the other day.

Yes! They were indeed the same boxes.

With a closer observation, I learnt that there was no lock or strong chain for their safety. So that was it.

At that very moment, I decided that it would be a brilliant idea to loot this Government money.

I studied the Railway time-table in detail, and found that the train under target starts from Saharanpur. I made a mental calculation, and assumed the amount available in the treasury to be minimum ten thousand rupees. I was evoked by this idea and shared it with my groupmates soon, who welcomed the thought enthusiastically.

Everyone supported my idea, and I was very excited. Ashfaq always followed my instructions like a disciple. It was really strange and unbelievable that he disagreed to the suggestion of the train robbery. I assumed that he foresaw the implications.

"We are not a very strong organisation as yet. This is like taking the British Government head-on. Yes, there is a big money coming in, but think about the risk we are taking, and what we may lose as a result."

I let him talk further. "What is your idea, Ashfaq?"

"We must continue to work without creating any doubts for the British Police, and focus on making our organisation stronger. If we come out in open now, not only us, but the revolutionaries from all over the country will be in trouble. It can shatter the force of the revolutionaries."

Looking back, I now realise that Ashfaq was absolutely correct and had a proper vision.

But at that moment, I acted adamant, since all the others were on my side. I did not believe in going back, once I took a decision.

On the other hand, Chandra Shekhar Azad appreciated the idea very much. He was very excited.

"We are not afraid of anyone. Let there be the Station Master, or his staff or even the Gora log. We shall kill them."

I admired the strength and determination of Azad, but we did not want any killings in this mission.

I said emphatically, "We will not kill anyone. We are only concerned with the Government money on the train. If we kill anyone, it is more likely that the person will be an Indian, so we will be killing our own countrymen."

Everyone agreed upon this point. Then the plan was worked out.

> *During the planning we realised, that even if we stop the train at a small station, capture the wire station (communication) and run away with the treasury money, we would require many more hands for the whole operation, since there would be considerable number of station staff, over and above the Railway Guards and engine drivers.*

It was unanimously decided that we would pull the chain half- way, while the train is in motion, and then loot the entire treasury.

We also considered that for pulling the emergency chain, the passengers should be travelling by the second class and not the third, since one can not rely on the chains working well in third class boggies.

Initially the plan was to be executed on the 8th of August, 1925. All the team members gathered at Lucknow.

They were staying separately and appeared dispersed, to avoid any attention by the police.

Some stayed at the reliable places like a guest house, temple, or an acquaintence's place in Lucknow. The majority stayed at the Chedilal Dharamshala (resthouse), but in different rooms.

At the pre-arranged time, everyone started reaching the Lucknow station.

No sooner did the group that started from the Chedilal Dharamshala reached the Lucknow station, then they saw a train leaving the platform.

Which train was this? Their detective found out that it was the same train that they were supposed to board – 8 down Express. Alas! They were late by 10 minutes.

> *Thus, our first attempt had failed. Since nothing was left to be done now, everyone returned to their respective destination feeling helpless and disappointed.*

Incidentally, a few days earlier, the group had an opportunity to meet Govind Kar, a senior freedom fighter.

He had fought face to face with the British Police at Pabna in Bengal, after which he was caught and sent to the Cellular Jail in the Andaman Nicobar Islands, and was released after serving the sentence for many years.

He was lying on a cot with his body covered, at a friend's place. As he removed the sheet, everyone could see innumerable wounds on his body.

We all were speechless. Govind Kar laughed dryly.

As he spoke, his words were filled with pain, "My body is covered with the wounds given with the knives, But think about our mother, Hindmata, who is suffereing so gravely and is in unbearable pain. Unlike me, she can't show it to anyone."

He started crying, "My pain is nothing as compared with what our mother - our homeland is going through."

He added sadly, "Sorry I can not be of any help now, but please do something to liberate our motherland, from the Britishers' hands who are looting and torturing her. Please do something!"

We could see that he was in terrible pain, and perhaps would not live any longer, suffering due to the beastly tortures inflicted upon him at the cellular Jail. But his words continued to echo into our ears for a long time, making our determination stronger to go ahead with this plan at any cost. There was no going back now.

The 9th August, 1925

For us, now it was a situation of 'Do or Die!' The next day was the 9th August— D-day for us, and this was final try.

By the early afternoon, the whole team embarked upon a train going towards the West, and got down at the station prior to Kakori. Once bitten, we were twice shy, nothing should go wrong now.

Ashfaq Ulla Khan, Rajendra Nath Lahiri, and Shachindra Nath Bakshi bought the second-class tickets and boarded the train.

The other seven – Keshav Chakravarti, Murailal, Mukundi Lal, Chandra Shekhar Azad, Banvari Lal and Manmath Nath Gupta, and me (Pandit Ramprasad Bismil)- spread ourselves maintaining distance, from one end of the train to the other.

At a pre-arranged time, the three revolutionaries sitting in the second-class compartment pulled the emergency chain. All this worked as per the plan.

The dusk had already set in, which was in our favour, since it would be difficult for the Police to recognise our faces or identify any of us.

As the train stopped, other groupmates who had spread themselves in the third class boggies, jumped down with pistols in their hands.

Everyone was delegated a specific task, and accordingly, they started operating.

Penned by ShachindraNath Bakshi

Since Ashfaq continued to plead Ram Bismil for dropping the idea of a rail loot, he was not given any particular task. Hence, Panditji put all the responsibility on my shoulders to carry out the action plan.

I told Panditji that I will board the second class compartment with Ashfaq (Ulla Khan) and Rajendra (Nath Lahiri), and once the train stopped, we will all descend and I would catch hold of the guard immediately.

Panditji liked this idea. He said that the remaining seven of us would disperse ourselves in other compartments and eventually meet when the train stopped.

I went to the ticket window at Kakori station to buy three second class tickets to Lucknow.

The assistant Station Master looked very surprised as who would buy the second-class tickets from such an insignificant station. I noticed this, and started looking in the other direction, pretending to wipe my face with a handkerchief, till he gave the tickets and remaining change.

Once we were on the railway platform, I called Ashfaq and Rajendra to be with me. Soon the train arrived. We looked for a vacant second-class compartment and sat down.

As soon as the train picked up speed, one passenger came and sat next to me. I tried to act nonchalant and pretended to look out of the window. After some time, when we reached beyond a distant signal, I asked my friends casually, “Where is the Jewel box?”

Ashfaq immediately replied, “Oh, I seem to have forgotten it at Kakori!”

As soon as he said this, I got up and pulled the emergency chain. Rajendra Lahiri did likewise from the other side. I immediately went near the compartment door, opened it and stood at the door.

The train stopped with a screeching sound. All three of us got down quickly and started walking in the direction of Kakori. We met the Railway Guard a little further, who asked, “Who pulled the chain?”

Then he waved for us to wait there. I replied, "I have forgotten my box at Kakori, so I am going to get it.'

By then all the other groupmates from the third-class compartment had descended and gathered there. We stopped near the guard's boggie.

We cautioned the passengers by firing a few bullets into the air from our pistols, and announced that no one should get down from the train. We did not want to harm anyone, but were only looting the Government treasury.

At that point, I saw the guard showing a green signal. I put my pistol on his chest and snatched his signal lamp.

I shouted at him, "How dare you do this? I will kill you."

He folded his hands and requested lamely, "Please spare me my life."

I pushed him again to lie down on the ground and warned, "Lie down on the grass with your face down."

Just then Panditji pulled me aside and cautioned, "Prabhas, the guard can see your face clearly in this light. Be careful."

There was no more daylight outside and thankfully it was difficult to identify anyone. All the other groupmates got hold of the iron box and pulled it down on the ground from the guard's bogie.

After being cautioned, none of the passengers dared to look at us or ask any questions.

Now we began to force open the treasury box. A hammer was kept ready for this purpose. The two group mates were standing on each side with the Mauser pistols in hand. We did not have rifles or revolvers for this loot.

*[**An interesting narration is well written by ShachindraNath Bakshi in his book 'Kranti ke path par' – The Guard remained faithful to his words till the end and did not ever identify Shachin da while interrogation of the revolutionaries was going on. This saved Shacnindra Nath Bakshi's life.]*

Interestingly, there was a British Major travelling by this train, who was equipped with an enfield/field revolver, and a few policemen who were carrying weapons too.

Thus, it was not unlikely that our sole purpose of looting the Government treasury might convert into an actual fight with the British Police anytime.

Breaking open of the iron chest was taking longer than we had expected. The box was very strong and would not break open in spite of our repeated attempts.

Ashfaq was given task of taking care of the passengers, but since none of them attempted to give a fight, he did not have much to do.

As he saw that the breaking open of the treasury box was taking longer than expected, he gave his pistol to Manmath (Nath Gupta), took the hammer from his groupmate and started attempting to open the chest.

Ashfaq was strong and heavily built like Ram Bismil. All the others were young boys in their 20s, including Azad.

Ashfaq attempted with full force and made strong blows with the hammer. In no time he broke open the upper lid of the chest. The eagerly awaited treasure started peeping out!

Unfortunately, the sound of the hammer was clearly heard in the quiet night from a long distance, which was obvious to happen.

Before we could heave a sigh of relief, the sound of an approaching train could be heard distinctly. It was not very far off. Everyone was shocked with disbelief.

What if that train stopped to find out why this train had halted midway?

Did anyone inform the railway authorities or the police about us? We were nonplussed and no one could speak anything.

The only thing our group could do was to stand still and face the consequences, whatever they might be.

Bismil da did not believe in any killings. It did not mean that he was against using the weapons to fight against the British. If the need may arise, then we might have to make use of our pistols and the other weapons.

Panditji said that this was the time for the Punjab Mail to pass by, and hopefully it might continue to do so.

As the train light approached and came very near, he instructed us, 'Hide your pistols! Ashfaq, throw away the hammer! All of you, stand still where you are!'

The train was very close, and in no time passed with the same speed as it would otherwise, without causing us any harm.

As soon as the Punjab Mail was some distance away, Ashfaq picked up the hammer and started attempting with all the more stronger blows again. Once the box opened, the money bags were collected rapidly.

We had to take another route for returning to avoid the eyes of the Police. Hence, we walked through the fields this time, and entered Lucknow from the Chowk area. Incidentally, this being a red-light area, people seemed to be on the roads till late night so we were safe with our mission accomplished.

After we collected the money, we tied it up in three separate packets, and started towards Lucknow.

The leather bags carrying the money were thrown into small water canals. The weapons were returned to their original place and the money was safely hidden. However, there was not much money that we had obtained from this loot, it was about five thousand rupees. *(There are different references to this amount: from five thousand to ten thousand rupees)* But this gave us an immense confidence to fight against the British Government face to face.

Everyone went back to their pre-destined places as if nothing had happened. Azad slept in a park, since he did not have any relative or a place to stay for the night.

While we were returning, Ram Bismil asked to check if anyone had forgotten their personal belongings at the loot spot, but no one remembered anything at that time. However, there was a shawl dropped on the tracks by one of the groupmates, which turned out to be quite a proof for the police later to track the involved revolutionaries.

We later learnt that there were fourteen passengers who had weapons of one or the other kind. But no one tried to give us a fight, which made the things easy for us, and much time and efforts were saved.

One passenger was killed, which could have been avoided. When the iron box was being broken, unfortunately one passenger got down from his compartment to meet his wife who was a little distance away in the train in the ladies' compartment. Manmath Nath thought that he was coming to attack, and fired at him.

Much later it was realised that the passenger had died on the spot.

The next morning the news vendors shouted aloud the headlines of the Indian Daily Telegraph '-Breaking News: Thrilling News – Government Treasure looted at Kakori.'

News ran thus:

'From Our Special Correspondent: Gorakhpur.

As per the news received, yesterday evening around 8 pm, few decoits with guns suddenly stopped the 8 Down train travelling from Hardoi to Lucknow by pulling the emergency chain and looted the Government treasury lying in the Guard's boggie.

The dacoits managed to run away. The police detectives are following their trails.

It is believed that there were around 30-40 involved in this loot. As soon as the train stopped, they warned no one to get off the train or would be shot. They said that their purpose was to loot the Government treasury only.

One eye-witness mentioned that few persons with rifles were guarding the train from both the sides, and firing bullets at regular intervals.

The Railway Guard was asked to lie face down on the ground.'

The news was getting more precise, 'We have learnt from the Police sources that this was not a dacoit attack, but the work of an international group.

When the Police reached the spot, they found only a hammer, safe box, broken knob and a shawl which are now in police custody. Dacoits seemed to have run away with treasury money.

The revolutionary groups were reading the news regularly but were not worried, as there was no likely clue to be found in this case.

Gradually, one by one, all returned to their respective hometowns.

With the money obtained, the pending debt on the revolutionary group was paid off and some money was sent to the branches of the 'HRA' in different cities. Left over money after buying the new weapons could be spent later.

The things had started to appear normal as far as the revolutionaries were concerned, but it was not exactly so. On the other side, the British Police had become very alert and had decided to follow this case more carefully and seriously.

Mr Harton, a British police officer was in charge of this case.

He started his probe by visiting the place where the loot had taken place and studied everything in detail.

It was already assumed that this was the act of revolutionaries, and as the investigation progressed, it was getting more and more obvious and clear.

As a result, the British Police arrested many suspects from Northern India.

Though there were only 10 revolutionaries involved, more than 40 suspects were arrested, mainly from Shahjahanpur, Benaras, Kanpur, Lucknow, Meerut, Agra and Allahabad and were duly imprisoned.

The British Police knew well how to extract information from the dedicated young patriots.

Shahjahanpur was always known for the revolutionary activities against the British from the beginning, which was the home town of Ram Prasad Bismil, Ashfaq Ulla Khan and many other revolutionaries in the group.

A group of policemen in plain clothes apprehended a young boy named Indu Bhushan. He was a student at the Government school, and used to help Panditji by receiving the posts from various centres of the revolutionaries and 'HRA'.

After tracking his activities, all the letters that he had received were confiscated, which helped the Police to learn many stories about the attacks and meetings to be carried out in the revolutionaries' owned 'HRA' group.

The principal of the school and Indu Bhushan were summoned to provide a copy of each correspondence.

Eventually, extreme intimidation broke Indu Bhushan down and he yielded to the pressure and became a government witness and gave away all the information that he had.

Ramesh Pandey, who used to receive Ramprasad Bismil's posts was also arrested from Benaras.

In less than a month, the series of arrests took place includingthat of Mukundi Lal.

It took almost a year to arrest Ashfaq and me (Shachindra Nath Bakshi). Next victim was Kudan Lal Gupta, who was arrested also during the Lahore Conspiracy.

Penned by ManmathNath Gupta

'Ashfaq was very clear in his concepts that our other objectives should not be mixed up with the prime object of securing funds. Presently the party was too weak to engage itself in a frontal battle with the regime, so it should continue to avoid the lime-light and build itself quietly.

Ashfaq proved to be right. The train hold-up, especially our announcement that we did not want to loot the passengers, but only Government property, shot the almighty British Government in the pit of its stomach. The whole infernal machine at once sprung into action.

I was one of the prime suspects in Benaras. Formerly, the police used to keep an eye on me, but now a day and night watch had begun. It was being openly commented that I was involved in the train hold-up. Owing to this, we shot into prominence among the youth of Varanasi. This proved to be a double-edged weapon. The youth in large numbers were eager to join the party, which made our work more difficult, because now there was a greater risk involved of some blacksheep smuggling himself into the party.

All were alerted that we should be cautious about the new entrants. Every person's whereabouts should be thoroughly checked and cross checked. The party was developing into an imposing mass in no time. A revolutionary party can not be judged by the number of its members only.

It becomes strong or weak, with the number of only such members who can run into the face of death at short notice.

The number of such members at Benaras was not more than 60, although the membership had gone upto hundreds. The 'Revolutionary Literature' was in great demand, but there was a dearth of such literature in Hindustani, and as our work mainly concentrated on Hindi speaking people, consequently the work suffered.

In the meanwhile, the British Government announced a reward of Rs.5000/- to the person giving a clue for arresting the culprits.

This announcement augmented the sensation. It was pasted on all the notice boards of the Railway Stations as well as at all Police Stations.

The public did not know anything about the hold up except reports that had appeared in the newspapers, but its sympathies were apparent. Antipathy towards the Government was so intense that even if anybody threw pebbles at the statue of the King or any of the well- known personality, he would be hailed as a hero. Had we been allowed to stay out of prison only six more months to consolidate our gains, there would have been no doubt that the party would have grown tremendously. But the thousand-headed hydra of the British bureaucracy proved smarter and more alert on this occasion.'

After Indu Bhushan, who unfortunately turned a Crown witness, Banvari Lal was arrested. As a result, things got much easier for the British Police. The CID got further information, and the Police attacked the places near Dakshineshwar in Calcutta, where a lot of bomb-making material was found, along with seven revolvers, pistols etc.

Rajendra Lahiri, one of the prime suspects of the Kakori Conspiracy was arrested from there.

Indu Bhushan was a student, helping Ram Bismil with letters to be sent to and received from the other Revolutionary centres.

Again through application of torture and threatening tactics, the police could trace many revolutionaries, via school principal. The next target was Ram Krishna Khatri.

Pranvesh Chatterji was arrested from Jabalpur and Shachindra Nath Sanyal who was already in the jail, was sent to Lucknow, assuming that he was also a part of the 'Kakori Conspiracy.'

The arrest of Jogesh Chandra Chatterji in October 1925, turned out to be greatly beneficial for the Government.The Police found two letters from him which bore list of all the groups in North India and 22 other districts where the revolutionary work was going on. He was sent from Hazaribaug to Lucknow. Govind Charan Kar was also arrested along with him.

None of Bismil's friends who used to work with him came to meet him after he was arrested or were not allowed to meet him. Thus, he was deprived of meeting any of his friends, and virtually was forced to cut off from the outside world.

The 4th January, 1926

The 'Kakori Conspiracy' case trial began on this day. 28 persons were tried in total. Jyoti Dixit and Virbhadra Tiwari were released. Two other turned witnesses and other three ran away, so a total of 21 accused were put on trial.

They were charged for the following crimes:

1. Dafa (Penal code no.)121 – Revolt against King Emperor
2. Dafa 369 – Dacoity and looting people's and Government money
3. Dafa 302 – Killings.

**dafa (clause or article *)*

Besides they were held responsible for many crimes that they didn't commit. The copy of the indictment was also not provided to the accused.

The accused were also not allowed to appoint lawyers they required and were rightfully eligible for.

Before the trial began, the accused were imprisoned without the trial being carried out for months and being unnecessarily delayed, and were brutally tortured in the jail, which can not be described in a few pages and in mere words...(this is something to be empathically felt).

The proceedings went on for one and a half years. From the Government's side, Pandit Jagat Narayan Mulla faught the case, who was paid Rs.500 per day.

The people however, were ready to help Ram Bismil's group. The leaders of the United Provinces, Pandit Govind Vallabh Pant, Chandrabhan Gupt, Mohan Lal Saxena etc. were there to support the accused.

The Government spent more than ten lakh rupees on the proceedings of this case.

On the other hand, none of the accused received any financial help from the leaders of the nation, or the people of India.

Not only that, Banvari Lal had the audacity to say in the court that Ram Bismil was running his household with the loot money.

Ram Bismil was a person with foresight and wisdom. He had written his own case defence. When it was read out in the court, everyone was surprised to see its precision and arguments. Even the British were impressed to see that he could write so well in a lawful language.

However, this went against him. Unfortunately, he was labelled as a very dangerous revolutionary and was destined to be a prisoner. On the 6th April 1926, the Session Court gave the verdict. Ram Bismil, Rajendra Lahiri and Roshan Singh were given death sentence.

In the meanwhile, Ashfaq Ulla Khan was arrested from a hotel in Delhi. This was followed by the arrest of Shachindra Nath Bakshi.

It was an easy task for the British to run a case against these two. Ashfaq was accused of the same crime as Ramprasad Bismil and his groupmates and was given death sentence.

The Session Judge sentenced Shachindra Nath Sanyal and Shachindra Nath Bakshi to be imprisoned at the Cellular Jail in the Andaman Nicobar Islands.

Manmath Nath Gupta was sentenced to fourteen years imprisonment. Govind Charan Kar, Mukundi Lal, Jogesh Chatterji, Ramkumar Sinha and Ram Krishna Khatri got ten years' imprisonment.

Suresh Bhattacharya and Vishnu Swaroop Dubashish were given seven years' jail each. Pranavesh Chatterji, Ramdulare Trivedi, Prem Krishna Khanna, Ram Nath Pandey and Bhupendra Sanyal were given five years imprisonment.

Banvari Lal was imprisoned for five years, and Indu Bhushan was released, as both of them had turned Crown witness.

Chandra Shekhar Azad could not be caught till the end. However, Azad died at Alfred Park in Allahabad on the 27th February 1931. The Police trapped him in the park after Virbhadra Tiwari (his old companion who later turned traitor) informed them about his presence there. He was wounded in the process of defending himself and killed three policemen and wounded many others. After a long shootout, he succumbed to the injuries caused by the Police bullets.

On the 18th July 1927, Government requested the Avadh Chief Court for severe punishments for the others, who were not to be sent to the gallows. As a result, Jogesh Chatterji, Govind Kar and Mukundi Lal's punishment was increased from 10 years' imprisonment to the life term.

For Suresh Bhattacharya and Vishnu Sharan, it was increased from 7 years to 10 years. Manmath Nath Gupta was declared too young to be given more punishment.

An appeal was sent to the Governor of the State for reconsidering the judgement and for forgiveness, which was rejected.

Ram Bismil's father sent a request signed by about 250 Zamindaars, Rais, Honorary Magistrate to the Viceroy. Even 78 Councils of the state and legislative assembly members requested for the forgiveness as well.

Pandit Madan Mohan Malaviya tried to meet the Viceroy personally and appealed to reduce the punishment of death sentence for the four revolutionaries, but this was flatly refused.

A similar request was sent to the England's Privy Council, which was also rejected. This was the last possible resort, and it failed as well.

Ram Bismil mentioned in his autobiography, "I wanted to set an example (by sending it to the Privy Council) to my Countrymen not to ever rely on the British Courts."

Ram Bismil completed his autobiography only 2 days prior to his being sent to the gallows.

Outside the jail, Bhagat Singh, Shiv Verma, Chandra Shekhar Azad and the others desperately tried to save and help Ram Bismil and his team-mates to abscond, but they were not successful for some reason or the other.

On Monday, the 19th December 1927, Ram Bismil, Roshan Lal and Rajendra Lahiri were sent to the gallows in the Gorakhpur Jail, and on the same day, Ashfaq was sent to the gallows in the Faizabad Jail.

A Golden Chapter, blood soaked and marked with the unmatched martyrdom extended by the passionate and intense patriots in the history of India's freedom struggle thus came to an end.

Only if the revolutionaries had received support from the then leaders of India and their own comrades and co revolutionaries had not yielded or turned traitors the chapter must have been written differently or at least if their pleas of mercy against the death sentences were taken generously and humanly, India would have been richer in the knowledge about thousands of real heroes who lived, and died for the country's freedom without any hesitation and who wholeheartedly sacrificed everything including their own lives to earn us freedom, who deserve to remain an eternal inspiration for the youth of today and tomorrow and the future leaders of the prodigious country. VANDE MATARAM!

❑

A Short Summary

"History is the version of past events that people have decided to agree upon.."

–Napolean Bonaparte

India's independence has neither happened overnight, nor has it been possible by efforts of a handful of leaders.

Thousands of unknown Indians patriots have fought against the British forces and sacrificed their lives for the country. However, there is no mention of them in any of the History books.

With this disagreeable curiosity, I dived into searching stories of the unsung heroes of our country to embark upon a heroic "Kakori Train Loot " that took place on 9th August, 1925. It had shaken pillars of the British empire in India by surprising the Government and can be marked as the warning signal to leave our country.

Background of the story begins from the end of 1919. By then, there was a widespread political discontent against the British Government in India. The infamous massacre at Jaliyanwala Bagh by General Dyer had culminated in the Non-cooperation movement under Gandhiji's leadership, which was launched in September 1920.

Unity in the country was strengthened and long standing grievances of the toiling masses against the British as well as Indian masters got an opportunity to express their real feelings through it.

Sadly, the Non-cooperation Movement was withdrawn very soon on 10th March 1922. Its sudden death created an upheaval in the minds of people to witness birth of a large number of revolutionaries.

Revolutionary groups believed in armed fight against the ruling British. These groups were chiefly concentrated in Bengal, Maharashtra, Bihar, the United Provinces and Punjab.

However, it was an uphill task for them. During their fight, revolutionaries lived under the most horrifying circumstances. Staying away from their families, they were often imprisoned and brutally tortured, eventually climbing the gallows - one after the other, only to fade away from the pages of Indian History – leaving no signs of their existence in the chapters of India's freedom struggle!

All this information and pathos of it pushed my dream project ".....(New name) Destination Kakori: 9th August, 1925..." into reality. An imaginary story that portrays life experiences, hardships and struggles of revolutionaries like Manmathnath Ji Gupta, Shachindranath Ji Bakshi, Ramprasad Ji Bismil, (and his sister), and many other unsung heroes.

Activites of the revolutionaries are woven along with many real incidences, one of which is to loot money from various sources for survival, when eventually, Ramprasad ji Bismil and his team-mates plan to loot the Railway treasury.

The characters in the story are Mukund Pandey, Satish Gupta, Banvari Gupta, Leela (Gupta) Pandey and Birendra Sharma, who symbolize the real martyrs and were sacrificed for teaming for the Kakori Train Loot. The story tries to portrays mental agony, dilemma and survival issues of people in those times.

The thrilling events which take place during this adventure are nail biting, in the story as well as in reality. It has been adopted after an exhaustive research and references from the books by various freedom fighters.

(New name) "Destination Kakori: 9th August, 1925" is a humble tribute to the unsung heroes of India who sacrified themselves for independence of our country !

Jai Hind !

The great Martyrs of Kakori Conspiracy

Shaheed Smarak, Kakori

❑